◎ 本书出版得到2017年中央高校建设一流大学(学科)和特色发展引导专项资金(项目号3017008121)及中央高校基本科研业务费专项资金(项目号2242016R30018)资助

合并、扩招、质量保障政策与创新：
一所中国重点大学的案例研究

Amalgamation, Expansion, Quality Assurance and Innovations:
A Case Study on a Key University in China

by

Jingning Zhang

张静宁 著

东南大学出版社
SOUTHEAST UNIVERSITY PRESS
·南京·

图书在版编目(CIP)数据

合并、扩招、质量保障政策与创新：一所中国重点大学的案例研究／张静宁著．—南京：东南大学出版社，2017.10

ISBN 978-7-5641-7384-5

Ⅰ.①合… Ⅱ.①张… Ⅲ.①高等教育—教育改革—研究—中国 Ⅳ.G649.21

中国版本图书馆 CIP 数据核字（2017）第 197134 号

合并、扩招、质量保障政策与创新：一所中国重点大学的案例研究

著　　者	张静宁
责任编辑	刘　坚
电　　话	(025)83793329/83790577(传真)
电子邮件	liu-jian@seu.edu.cn
出版发行	东南大学出版社
出 版 人	江建中
地　　址	南京市四牌楼2号
邮　　编	210096
销售电话	(025)83794561/83794174/83794121/83795801/83792174/83795802/57711295(传真)
网　　址	http://www.seupress.com
电子邮件	press@seupress.com
经　　销	全国各地新华书店
印　　刷	虎彩印艺股份有限公司
开　　本	700mm×1000mm　1/16
印　　张	14.75
字　　数	300千字
版　　次	2017年10月第1版第1次印刷
书　　号	ISBN 978-7-5641-7384-5
定　　价	40.00元

* 未经本社授权，本图书内任何文字不得以任何方式转载、演绎，违者必究。

* 本社图书若有印装质量问题，请直接与营销部联系。电话:025-83791830。

Abstract

The Chinese higher education reform policies since 1993 have been pursued in a centralized, top-down manner, which some theorists characterize as "centralized decentralization" or governmental "steering at distance." This case-study research has two purposes. First, is to evaluate the implementation or the "situated practices" of national higher education reform policies (the amalgamation, expansion, and quality assurance policies). Second, is to elaborate on the locally-grounded innovative ideas and practices at a key university in a large city in China. The methodological approach used is phenomenological interviews, a vehicle that elicits "local knowledge" and accords the status of expertise to the interview participants. This methodology maps out the different experiences and meanings that different social groups derive from the centralized policies and generates new ideas for policy actions.

The findings suggest that at the institutional level, the faculty members, administrators, and students are highly reflexive, resilient and pragmatic. Instead of mutely accepting national higher education reform policies as given, the faculty members, administrators and students are making an active effort to reappropriate distant faculty members, fashioning them into locally meaningful and relevant terms and practices. Furthermore, the findings suggest that small-scale, inside-out innovations grounded in local people's meaning-making systems and congruent with their perceptions of organizational purposes, profuse and proliferate at the university of focus.

In conclusion, in this study, I stress the importance to distinguish universities which naturally defy top-down, centralized reform efforts, and other models of organizations (e. g., business organizations and annexations of governmental bureaus). Furthermore, I discuss the viability of inside-out, bottom-up approaches to policymaking in higher education reforms.

Table of Contents

Chapter 1   Introduction ··· 1
   Statement of Problem ··· 4
   Objectives and Significance of the Study ························ 16
   Defining the Case ·· 20
   Overview of the Research ····································· 23

Chapter 2   Literature Review ································· 26
   Amalgamation and Expansion ································· 27
   Chinese National Quality Assurance Policies ···················· 55

Chapter 3   Methods ··· 70
   Setting ·· 70
   Researcher Positionality ······································ 74
   Participants ··· 79
   Data Collection and Analysis ·································· 84

**Chapter 4   University People's Experiences and Perceptions
of the Amalgamation and Expansion Polices**
··· 94
   Experiences with and Resistance to the Amalgamation Policy
··· 95
   Experiences with and Perceptions of the Expansion Policy ··· 109
   Summary ·· 130

Chapter 5 University People's Experiences and Perceptions
           of Quality Assurance Mechanisms ········· 132
   Experiences with and Perceptions of the National Undergraduate
      Teaching Evaluation ···································· 134
   The Uinversity's Dudao Team and Faculty Coping Strategies
      ·· 147
   Research Promotion Criteria and Faculty Coping Strategies ··· 153
   Summary ·· 166

Chapter 6 Innovative Ideas and Practices at the University
           of Focus ·· 167
   Five Properties of Local Innovations ···························· 169
   Summary ·· 184

Chapter 7 Conclusions and Implications ················ 185
   Summary of the Previous Chapters ····························· 185
   Implications ·· 190

References ·· 201

Chapter 1
Introduction

There is no denial of the remarkable achievements of Chinese higher education (HE) reform since the economic reform in 1978, especially after the watermark year of 1993, in which the passage of *The Outlines of Chinese Education Reform and Development* (hereafter *Outlines*) was agreed to be a turning point (Ministry of Education [MoE], 1993). Yet the problems inherent in the reform process do not escape critics' scrutiny. In today's global society, a superpower is no longer defined by the size of national armies or possession of nuclear weapons, but by "the size and prestige of university system" (Baker, 2007). Chinese HE, benefited from governmental constant investment and shrewd reform strategies, not only grows a capability to serve domestic needs, but also gradually elevates itself out of its chronicle "giant-periphery" status in the world's knowledge system (Altbach, 1981, 2001, 2004).

Indictors of such growth are numerous. To name just a few, by 2004, China had the largest HE system in the world, "with 19 million students enrolled in universities, adult education, private (minban) institutions and distance learning programs" (Mohrman, 2008). The enrolments of Ph. D. students, an indicator of a university system's research capacity, were 34,000 in 2006, and are expected to surge past 50,000 in just three or four years, overtaking the current world's leader, the United States. Besides, China has three universities in top 100 plus another two if one includes Hong

Kong. In 2005, one of the Chinese flagship universities, Beijing University, had replaced the University of Tokyo as the highest-ranking Asia-Pacific university, according to the *Times Higher Education Supplement* (Yonezawa, 2007). Furthermore, Chinese universities have been increasingly internationalized, turning into a relatively inexpensive and adjacent destination for further education for students from Asia whereas its possibility to attract students from other parts of the world, such as North America and Europe, is inestimable. In the year of 2005, there were 140,000 international students in China, a 27.28% increase than in 2004 (MoE, 2009b; Shambaugh, 2004/2005; T. Wang & X. M. Liu, 2006; Ye & Xiao, 2007). All the seemingly random evidence points to the enormous growing capacities of Chinese universities, and is constantly cited as counterexamples to the "center-periphery" theories developed by Altbach and others (Altbach, 1981, 2001, 2004; Gopinatha & Altbach, 2005; R. Yang, 2002).

Despite its success, critics constantly point out the problems inherent in the reform process. A plethora of recent literature assessing gains and losses of Chinese HE reform centers on three broad realms of concern: (a) the transition from the elite to mass HE, (b) the integration and differentiation of HE system (e. g., the appearance of "autonomous" institutions), and (c) the changing relationship between the government and universities, with attendant concerns of university governance and authority (e. g., Dong, 2004, 2005; Huang, 2005; Kang, 2000, 2005; H. C. Wang, 2004; Mohrman, 2005, 2008; R. Yang, 2004). The third area attracts most critical attention, as the disparate Chinese social-political traditions have given rise to the unique government-university dyad, a lack of institutional autonomy and academic freedom at the university level that stands in stark contrast to the experiences of Western "core" countries (Hayhoe, 1996). One line of Sinological literature tends to find sources in Chinese indigenous scholarship for the explanation of this phenomenon. Hayhoe for instance, argues that the values and structures associated with traditional Chinese higher learning institutions have persisted and informed struggles and conflicts in the development of HE right up to the present time. In the traditional society before the abolition of the Civil Service Exam in 1905, education (e. g. the Civil Service exam) was the means to ascending political power, and the ruling class was able to control its servants by defining what valuable knowledge was. When Western-style learning institutions were transplanted and grafted on top of a highly sophisticated indigenous scholarship system in the late 19th century, they tended to be viewed as an instrument of the State, and be annexed to state bureaucratic apparatus as traditional institutions of higher learning were (see also Bastid, 1987; Curran, 2005; Hartnett, 1996; Pepper, 1996; Weston, 2004).

More recent literature on Chinese HE reform, however, started to examine the uneasy coexistence of and tensions between a state-controlled HE system and the emergence of a market controlling mechanism in the neoliberal context (Hawkins, 2000; Law, 1996; Mok, 1997, 2001, 2004, 2005a, 2005b, 2007a, 2007b; R. Yang, 2002, 2004; R. Yang, Vidovich, & Currie, 2007), as critics point out that the fundamental assumption is that an authoritarian political system can coexist in harmony with a free market. The problems might not be manifest during earlier phase of the reform, but are becoming increasingly acute and in dire needs of attention in the current national policy context of favoritism, and post-WTO international competitions (Bao & R. Liu, 2002).

This case-study research follows the second venue of literature related to the contradictions between the bureaucratic and market controlling systems and highlights the uneasy government-university relationship through a specific angle, the analysis of the *ideologies*, *processes* and *effects* of national HE reform policies. By thoroughly examining national HE reform policies, the readers can have a clear understanding of, despite the rhetoric of "decentralization", how two types of independent entities, the national governmental bodies (MoE in this case) and universities interact with each other, and how one is apt to deploy, annex and steer the other to achieve goals that fit into the broader nation-building picture. This case-study research—the attempt to study the implementation of HE reform policies (amalgamation, expansion, quality assurance mechanisms) and the innovative change initiatives in a single university organization—will be based on this anatomy of the problematic government-university dyad.

Statement of Problem

I will first define policy *ideologies*, *processes*, and *effects*, and explain why they help us understand the government-university dyad in face of the emerging market controlling mechanism of HE. I will then proceed to argue that national HE reform policies are neoliberal-ideology driven, which has both negative and positive consequences. However, in China the highly centralized policy processes are fundamentally discrepant with the ideologies underlying national HE reform policies, a fact that tends to amplify the negative and eliminate the positive side of neoliberal ideology. Given this understanding, questions profuse as to what effects national HE reform policies can achieve. The problematic government-university dyad, as is manifested in the analysis of national HE reform policies, gives rise to the necessity of this particular case study first on the "situated practices" of national HE reform policies and then on the innovative practices, the inside-out, bottom-up change forces at the university of focus.

Policy *ideologies* are the "taken-for-granted understandings that constitute parameters for what is legitimate—that is, what is expected, appropriate and sacred, as well as the converse" (Gumport, 2000, p. 71). They explain what rationales are given for the policymaking; who stands to benefit from the policy, and if there are deeper purposes being served by the policy, etc. Policy *processes* refer to who participate, and how the policy objects are designed and formulated. Policy *effects* refer to the implementation: How policy practitioners and those at the "receive end" of the policy interact to bring about or fail to bring about the stipulated policy goals. By thoroughly examining the ideologies, processes and effects of national HE reform policies, I will demonstrate how the two types of independent entities, national governmental bodies (MoE in this particular case) and universities interact with each other, and how the latter is conceptualized, positioned and steered by the former to achieve goals that fit into the broader nation-building picture.

National HE reform policy ideologies

Situated in the context of corporate or capitalist globalization (Olssen, 2004; Went, 2000), Chinese HE since 1993 has been neoliberal-ideology driven; that is, it is the quest for economic efficiency, effectiveness, economy, productivity that dominates policy discourses, as Slaughter and Rhoades (2004) lament that educational policies no longer stand on their own right, but are treated as subsets of economic policies (see also Mok, 2004; Torres & Rhoads, 2006; Torres & Schugurensky, 2002; R. Yang, 2002). Since 1978 when it started to shift from its isolationist, politics-oriented policies to outward-looking, economy-oriented policies, China has been "enthusiastically and actively" engaged in the global process (Vidovich, R. Yang, & Currie, 2007). The period of 1993 and 2009, the time frame in which HE reform policies in this case study (amalgamation, expansion and quality assurance mechanisms) set in, witnessed a deepening of global impacts on HE reform initiatives and drives. Such effects are achieved through conscious and active borrowing, the "mimetic" processes whereby China seeks to imitate the practices of countries perceived to be successful (e.g., building "world-class" universities), as well as through inexorable and irresistible imposition, the "diffusion" of norms and values from "core" to "periphery"/ "semi-periphery" countries through various mechanisms (Green, 1997, 1999; McNeely, 1995; McNeely & Cha, 1994; Torres & Schugurensky, 2006; Mohrman, 2005, 2008; J. N. Zhang, 2006). For instance, Vidovich et al. maintain that there is "isomorphism" of educational policies in China and the United States, though not in policy details, at least in policy ideologies (see also Green, 1997).

Neoliberal policies have both negative and positive consequences. On the one hand, in neoliberal quest for economic rationality, universities are conceptualized in a simplistic and reductionist way, as engines of economy, as Scott and Harding (2007) state that "universities are to the 'information age' what coal mines and steel mills were to the industrial economy" (p. 3). Other competing social goods, such as quality, equity and democracy are rendered powerless in face of the addition to GDP brought about by technological transfer or student cost-sharing, as Torres and Schugurensky (2002) point out that governments "withdraw from [their] responsibility to administer public resources and from the liberal premise of pursuing egalitarianism, replacing them with a blind faith in the market and the hope that economic growth will eventually generate enough of a spillover to help the poor and disenfranchised" (p. 433). R. Yang (2004) comments that social justice issues are not the first priority for Chinese HE policies since 1993. The pursuit for economy and efficiency produces social weakeners, as "the group located at the bottom of social resource distribution with the lowest living standards, [who] are especially vulnerable to new policy pitfalls" (p. 175).

On the other hand, neoliberal reform advocates "deregulation," in which governments resign from the traditional role as providers and regulators of universities, and shift towards a "facilitator" role, fostering the free competition of different institutions in a deregulated market. Many theorists believe that market mechanism eliminates the pitfalls of traditional bureaucratic control of HE, and is an incentive for quality, efficiency, differentiation, and innovations at local institutions (Teixeira, Jongboled, Dill & Amaral, 2004; Vandenberghe, 1999). It is expected that, universities operating in financial stringencies and highly competitive market are more innovative, efficient and responsive to the needs of economy and societies. For instance, Vandenberghe (1999) argues that universities concerned with their economic survival in fierce competition with peers are not only carefully calculating spending but also motivated to generate resources in innovative ways. In a similar line, Clark (1998) exalts "entrepreneurial" university that "actively seeks to innovate in how it goes about its business… seeks to work out a substantial shift in organizational character so as to arrive at a more promising posture for the future… seeks to become 'stand-up' universities that are significant actors on their own terms" (p. 4). According to him, a university that embodies a "steering inner core" (e. g., self-organized teams and groups by faculty members, administrators, or students within a single university or across different universities) is capable of innovative revenue-generating practices, and survival or prospering, even if it is not protected by governmental funding as flagship universities. Following this venue of literature, many observers advocate and celebrate the "decentralization" of Chinese HE (Kang, 2005; Mok, 1997).

National HE reform policy processes

Whereas the ideologies underlying HE reform policies, and the legitimating ideas regarding what is good, expected and sacred, are enforcing a decentralizing system, the policy processes are highly centralized in China—some attribute this fact to the lingering effects of the comand economy; some trace back further in history, finding explanatory sources in indigenous scholarship tradition (Bastid, 1987; Hayhoe, 1996; Hartnett, 1996; Pepper, 1996; Weston, 2004; R. Yang, 2002; R. Yang et al., 2007). HE reform policies emanate from national (sometimes international) centers, and filter all the way down to the universities. Universities have been recast as economic resources, in need of being strategically deployed for national economic development or international competition. With very few exceptions (e.g., Beijing University and Qinghua University) (Kang, 2005; Y. Luo & F. G. Ye, 2005; S. Pan, 2007), changes are given to but not created within universities, as universities stay passively adrift in external forces of change. In other words, the policy processes tend to endlessly amplify the negative side of neoliberalism, emphasizing the efficient coordination of economic resources, while eliminating the positive side of neoliberalism, not allowing universities to acquire sufficient autonomy and steering power.

First, major HE reform policies are mandates of the MoE. They are pushed forward by "heroic" ministers, in a non-consensus seeking manner, forming national tidal waves of change and co-opting all universities, in spite of some universities' reluctance (Dong, 2004; Mohrman, 2005, 2008). Taking the major HE reform policies since 1993, amalgamation, expansion and national quality-assurance policies for example, Mohrman (2003) observes that during the tidal wave of amalgamation between 1992 and 2006, some reluctant universities experienced "'shotgun weddings' at the behest of government leaders." Y. M. Wan and Peterson (2007) lament that a proliferation of research emphasizes government's role in initiating, prescribing and regulating university mergers, while there is hardly any research devoting to describing an institutional perspective.

The expansion policy in 1999 received even more critical attention, as the decision to increase undergraduate enrolments by 42% in one year was made and enforced in a 4-month time frame by MoE, detached from universities' preparedness or the market's ability to absorb university graduates (D. M. Luo & J. Liu, 2008; Kang, 2000). Likewise, national teaching and research quality assurance mechanisms are adopted despite frontline academic staffs' virulent criticisms of and resistance against them (J. N. Zhang, 2010). Song and Liao (2004) comment that, in China, top political leaders' will and government intentions are more likely to be crystallized into policies. "We use the word 'project' to describe a policy...The word indicates central planning and political sloganeering. Such policies hardly grow out of the market logic; rather, they reflect government's will and intentions" (p. 26).

Moreover, national HE reform policies bear imprints of the World Bank's agenda, who is consulted or participates in drafting of national plans since Chinese substantial educational borrowing in the 1980s (Hayhoe, 1996; Jacobson & Oksenberg, 1990). The World Bank is famous for attaching project covenants—side conditions—to its purse, dictating reforms in borrower countries, despite its rigid views on education and development and its ignorance of the borrower countries' perspectives (Jones, 2007; J. Xu, 2006). Furthermore, the Bank's tremendous power in educational decision making is attributed to not only "its capacity to mobilize funds and to impose conditions" (Torres & Schugurensky, 2002, p. 438), but also its capacity in research: the expertise, analytic skills and experience of its professional staff, its capacity to collect data throughout the world, and its efficiency in distributing the documents to key educational and political leaders in developing countries.

The Bank more successfully engages China in a policy dialogue, as the authoritarian and centralized Chinese government is more able to enforce ministry edicts without fear of critical opposition parties and free press, as compared to "the quarrelsome, fractious, short-term, decentralized parties and democratic government of India" (Drake, 2001, p. 227). Y. Wang's (2001) research finds out a surprising congruence between the World Bank's policy suggestions on education and the actual policies adopted in China. The research cites eight areas where Chinese educational policies and the Bank's advocacy overlap, such as decentralization, amalgamation, student admission, student cost-sharing, accountability measures. J. Xu (2006) writes that "the Bank's suggestions are accepted and implemented wholesale as the first-priority mandates, although some Chinese leaders are skeptical about them. The ideas on efficiency and related practices… are faithfully adopted" (p. 15).

In short, most national HE reform policies bear the imprint of the World Bank's agenda. Some protector views maintain that the Bank "while influential, has not been the source of the reform program with which, after all, began before China's participation in the World Bank. Rather, there has been a convergence of views" (Drake, 2001, p. 225). However, stronger evidence suggests that the Bank has been the source of many HE reform initiatives which are several layers removed from the universities that are actually affected, as Torres and Schugurensky (2002) state that the "World Bank has become the most important single source of multilateral technical co-operation and the lead agency in setting the education and development agenda" (p. 438, see also Hayhoe, 1996; Task Force on Higher Education and Society, 2000; J. Xu, 2006; Y. Wang, 2001).

Some attribute the highly centralized policy processes to the lingering effects of the planned economy; Some trace back further in history, finding explanatory sources in indigenous scholarship tradition (Bastid, 1987; Hayhoe, 1996; Hartnett, 1996; Pepper,

1996; Sleeboom, 2004; Weston, 2004; R. Yang, 2002; R. Yang et al., 2007). R. Yang (2002) and R. Yang et al. (2007), have done prominent reviews on the history of Chinese HE, which reveals that modern Chinese universities were grafted on top of the scholarly traditions that were vastly different from the traditions on which Medieval European universities were predicated. Higher-learning institutions are naturally a part of state political apparatus. They are unequivocally thought of being in the national economic and political interest, and tend to be deployed by higher-level of government bureaus for such purposes.

More theorists attribute the highly centralized policymaking processes to the legacies of the planned economy that are contending and struggling for control, despite the neoliberal market-based HE reform (A. Ding & Levin, 2007; Fischer, 1990; J. Xu, 2006; R. Yang, 2002; R. Yang et al., 2007). Fisher maintains that the technocratic concepts, the reliance on trained experts for decision-making are an integral part of socialist countries, given the emphasis on comprehensive economic and social planning. It is likely that top political leaders and technocratic experts form policy coalitions, which leaves out the mass public on the basis of the public's lack of knowledge. Thus, decision making is inevitably concentrated on the top echelons of society and top down. This view is somehow echoed in Kang's (2000) comment that "decisions made by higher level of government tap better the whole picture and offer solutions to the major problems. When assessing the pros and cons of certain policies, the government makes sure that the pros outweigh and the majority benefit" (p. 31). He further argues that educational reform should be part of the "strategic blueprint of political economy and should be adapted to the development of economy and society" (p. 32).

Such government-and-experts-know-better mentality lingers on. J. Xu (2006), and A. Ding and Levin (2007) notice that unlike in Western developed countries where resources are coordinated among universities through a mature market, there are often centralized, political fiats and mandates that attempt to create or steer market behaviors, as A. Ding and Levin comment that "using its ultimate power, the strong State initiated a change in the domestic structure by introducing or creating a market economy… The market is the engine, but it is the State, not the invisible hand of the market, that directs the engine. The price is … political distortion of the market" (p.542). For instance, the undergraduate expansion policy in 1999 is accused of ignoring markets' ability to absorb university graduates (D. M. Luo & J. Liu, 2008). Kalsen (2000) uses the term "centralized decentralization" and Vidovich (2002) "steering at distance" to characterize Chinese government's attempt to achieve decentralizing goals through highly centralized policies.

National HE reform policy effects

Given the fundamental discrepancies in ideologies and processes of national HE reform policies, criticisms profuse as to what effects national HE reform policies achieve. The fact that the locus of HE reform policymaking is several layers removed from the universities is defeating the purposes of HE reform that focuses on decentralization and fostering university enterprising and local innovations in teaching, research, and administration. Furthermore, the highly centralized policy processes bear with them the assumption that policies are implemented in a social vacuum, that policy intentions and outcomes inevitably match, ignoring that universities, traditionally more "bottom heavy" than other social institutions, are too bottom-resistant for any tycoon to dominate.

First, critics pointed out that the processes of centralized policymaking and implementation and the purposes of the policies are defeating each other, so that HE reform is a paradox in that the means to achieve some ends contradicts the very ends themselves. The policymaking process stresses the "interventionary" role of the State, legitimating the State's role in initiating, prescribing and regulating any changes that occur at a university whereas the central goals of the reform embody purposes such as cultivating university enterprising, academic freedom, local innovations (Mok, 1997; 2005a). Ironically, the State as a central actor, in the process of enforcing these goals, restricts the possibility of their realization as well. Using O'Conner (1995)'s simple metaphor, the mode of HE policymaking is like the situation of a foreman who "asks employees to participate in the work process but who also struggles to control the work, which keeps his subordinates in passive roles" (p. 770). For instance, the purpose of HE reform is to strengthen universities' ability to respond to clients and compete with peers. However, the central government maintains a directing role in supervising universities' moving towards these goals as defined by the government. Continued top-down control and guidance prevent universities from implementing meaningful, situation-specific changes.

Second, some researchers question the efficiency and effectiveness of the normative content of national policies to influence the values and norms of organizational actors. That is, to what degree do national reform policies bring about changes in HE institutions? Traditionally, a university has been viewed as more "bottom-heavy" than other social subsystems; its functions naturally defy hierarchical structures (Clark, 1998; Gornitzka, Kyvik, & Stensaker, 2005), as is manifested in the familiar similes "herding cats", "moving graveyards" (Scott & Harding, 2007) or "organized anarchies" (Cohen & March, 1986). Although top-down policies might be relatively successful in steering organizational behaviors at the macro level, it is questionable regarding how governmental legislations and decrees are able to penetrate the inner core, in Owens' (1998) words, the "assumptions and structures" or "organizational cultures" of universities. He further states that top-town enforcement of HE reform policies might bring about overall changes in a time-efficient manner, but in the long run, universities have demonstrated considerable resilience in dealing with external forces for change by maintaining stability over time. Universities often frustrate even rigorous governmental efforts.

Corwin (1974) in his classic work holds the belief that national policy intents can be clearly stated, however, there is always a "slippage" between the levels where policies are formulated and where they are practiced. He says that "the longer the hierarchy, the more distortion that can take place at each successive lower level, due to misinterpretations as well as to conflicts of interest between subordinate and super-ordinate groups" (p. 256). Others concur with him by stating that policies, decrees and commands from without the university are "delayed, distorted, deflected and destroyed ... as often as [they are] faithfully implemented" (Delany & Paine, 1991, p. 26). Ownership of educational policies, then, becomes a key ingredient for the acceptance and success in practice. Barry (1999) suggests that change efforts emanated from the base, although slow in developing, are more likely to be effective because they are grounded in general acceptance. Hanson (1997) further concurs by stating that organizational change does not come with passing of laws or signing decrees. It is "built" rather than "created". He states that

> The organizational culture (e. g. the way we've always done things around here) must be transformed, new roles learned, leadership styles altered (e. g. shifting from controlling to supporting actions), communication patterns reversed, planning procedures

revised (e. g. bottom up and top down) and regional policies and programs developed. (p. 122)

Such change is grounded in wider, democratic participation of those whose lives are directly affected by the policy, rather than in coercive top-down enforcement of legislations.

In short, the cursory analysis of the *ideologies*, *processes*, and *effects* of national HE reform policies reveals the problematic government-university dyad, a tendency for the former to annex the latter to state political apparatus and strategically deploy the latter for political and economic purposes. In the neoliberal context, the State's legitimate role in initiating, prescribing and enforcing HE reform policies, has amplified the negative side of the economic rationality. Universities are characterized as some economic resources, a vehicle for achieving State's national economic goals and winning international competition. The positive side of neoliberalism, the romantic ideas of improving efficiency, quality, differentiation, innovation, as many theorists believe can be achieved through introducing a market-controlling system, is unreachable given the State superseding power over universities. Mok (2004) and R. Yang (2004) agree that despite the rhetoric of "decentralization," the State's role as "a regular and overall service coordinator has been strengthened rather than weakened" (Mok, 2004, p. 4). Similarly, Vidovich et al. (2007) comment that, "the State has gained power through repositioning itself as 'market manager', steering via different mechanism than in the past, steering very strongly all the same, on the assumption that it will serve 'the national interest'" (p. 104). While the universities in neoliberal contexts face more financial uncertainties as the State "pass the bucks down", they did not acquire corresponding self-steering power or autonomy in an environment of financial stringencies and fierce competition (Delany & Paine, 1991). Furthermore, the effectiveness and efficiency of national HE reform policies are constantly called into question, as people at universities constantly resist and behave deflectively. All these analyses suggest that despite the great success of HE reform between 1992 and 2009, it is problem-ridden as well.

Objectives and Significance of the Study

This research attempts to offer a point-to-point analysis on the problems outlined above. First, it evaluates national HE reform policies (amalgamation, expansion and quality assurance mechanisms), through their "situated practices" in the university setting. The question asked is how distance policies interface with the university, and are experienced, reconstituted or resisted by university people. Second, as Fairweather (1996) maintains that a university changes through adaptation to external forces and transitions (e. g. , economic change, national reform policies) as well as through inner debates, this case study focuses on local innovative practices and attempts to find alternatives to top-down, outside-in national policymaking.

There are two sets of research questions in this research.

1) How do national HE reform policies, amalgamation, expansion and quality assurance mechanisms, interface with the university of focus? How are these policies perceived and responded to by administrators, faculty members and students in their mundane duties and routines?

2) On the basis of the empirical findings of the first set of questions, are there alternatives to the centralized, top-down policymaking in HE? What practices are considered innovative and acceptable to universities people, and thus constitute an inner force for university change?

Chapter 1　Introduction

First, in this research I attempt to evaluate the implementation of national HE reform policies at a key university in China. I have argued before that in the national reform policymaking, universities are usually unequivocally thought of as in the national economic and political interest (Hayhoe, 1996; Hartnett, 1996; S. Pan, 2007). They are usually thought of as in need of being deployed strategically for national purposes, for instance, for the competition in the global economy, whereas universities' own perspectives are neglected and obscured in the national grand narratives of what is important for the universities and what they should be good for. The fundamental assumption in the traditional nation-centered, rational-purposive view on policy is that if each step of policymaking is guarded by scientific, objective, and uninterested data, then the natural corollary is that the outcomes of policy-implementation will match the original policy intentions and purposes, as if these policies were carried out in a social vacuum (Trowler, 2002). More recent literature on policy implementation challenges the assumptions in the centralized model in that the intensions and goals in policies made at a distance tend to be lost or distorted through the long chain of implementation, due to misunderstandings, deliberate distortions or the complexity of contexts where policies land (Corwin, 1974; Gornitzka et al., 2005; Sabatier, 2005; Rein & Schön, 1996).

In this case under study, the implementation of amalgamation, expansion and national quality assurance policies is carried out in a university setting which is characterized by a strong tradition of "bottom heaviness," "organized anarchism," "antagonist cultures," and professional autonomy and discretion (Bridgman, 2007; Cohen & March, 1986; Weick, 1976; Trowler, 1998, 2001, 2002, 2005). Newton (2002) argues that "a significant feature of policy implementation is the discretion exercised at the point of implementation by 'front-line' workers or street-level bureaucrats" (p. 49). What is expected is that, in receiving the policy, values and attitudes are much more "subtly diverse and unpredictable" (p. 43), and coping strategies and resistance profuse, as top-down policies "constrain but not construct" practices (Darling-Hammond, 1990, p. 341). Jones (2007) and Darling-Hammond maintain that people down the educational line, such as "street-level" bureaucrats and classroom teachers, play an active and dynamic role in reshaping, thus are a *de facto* integral part of top-down policymaking (see also Rein & Schön, 1996; Newton, 2002; Harvey & Newton, 2004). Therefore, educators' and administrators' experiences and reconstitution of the major national HE reform policies are in need of in-depth study. In cases where resistance is present, it should not be treated as problematic and in need of being overcome, but as an "appreciative focus", and a "social phenomenon requiring systematic inquiry and explanation" (Doyle & Ponder, 1977). In other words, according to Newton, it is necessary to account or describe university people's experiences with and resistance to national HE reforms policies in their own right, but not to "describe or explain them in order to correct them" (p. 48).

This research seeks to evaluate national HE reform policies by examining the implementation or "situated practices" of the national HE reform policies, amalgamation, expansion and quality assurance policies. The amalgamation started off around 1992 and continued into late 2006, which according to Mohrman's (2003) observation was co-opting all Chinese universities despite their complacency or reluctance. The "reactive growth" (Clark, 1996) of universities—the expansion of undergraduate enrolments, broaching in the year of 1999, was deemed "a Great Leap Forward" in HE development history, and was followed by a prospect of graduate enrolment expansion in 2008. Furthermore, quality assurance policies in teaching and research are a strong aspect of Chinese HE, as

Vidovich et al. (2007) comment that, in the past 20 years, Chinese governmental regulations and control of HE escalate in that "Chinese universities are subject to unprecedented external scrutiny" (p. 93). All policies have profound and lasting impacts on the landscape of HE today. Policies made outside of universities by politicians and technocratic experts on the basis of "scientific criteria" are constantly challenged in that they are several layers removed from those whose lives are really affected by those policies. Thus, it is necessary to evaluate how these policies are carried out and received by university people.

Second, this research hypothesized that despite the compelling totalizing tendencies in the national HE reform discourses, universities remain "active agents", and innovative centers of localized and grassroots organizational changes, albeit to different degrees. Ample theoretical fabrication or empirical evidence verifies and affirms this hypothesis in the literature depicting HE in Western the "core" countries. Weick (1976), Cohen and March (1986) and a great number of others (Geiger, 2004; Gornitzka, Kogan, & Amaral, 2005; Trowler, 2001, 2002, 2005) have argued theoretically that universities and colleges are naturally more decentralized than other social and lower-level educational institutions. Clark (1983, 1996, 1998) throughout his career persistently insists, through empirical findings that, change in HE emanates from activities at the base of the system. Building on this strong literature base, I hypothesized that innovative practices are embodied in university people's daily activities and that change agents reside within but not without the university. Thus I intend to test the hypothesis with rich empirical evidence collected from the university of focus, to avoid the fallacy of what Marginson and Considine (2000) criticize as "essentialist" approach, the tendency of discussing the universal "essence" of universities abstracted from their specific social-historical contexts. On the basis of empirical findings on the abundance and thriving of localized innovative practices, this research proposes bottom-up, inside-out changes as an alternative trajectory to top-down, centralized policymaking. As Weick (1976) proposes, although human creations, educational organizations, "loosely-coupled", acquire a life of their own. We should not project industrial processes onto educational organizations, making the organizations work the way as we plan, but see schooling as agriculture, in which we have to center our efforts around "what seeds, plants, and insects are likely to do anyway" (p.2).

Having laid out the overarching objectives of the case-study research, the question left to be answered is what is a case study?

Defining the Case

I define this research as a case study. First, I will define this research through its unit of analysis and by comparing it to other types of studies (e.g., statistical, experimental and historical). It is through defining what it is not that the characteristics of a case study become clear (Merriam, 1998; R. Yin, 2003). Second, I will argue that the university of focus is a "typical" or "representative" case among many other available cases. Third, although R. Yin and Merriam state that a case study "does not claim any particular methods for data collection or data analysis" and can be both quantitative or qualitative, I will argue that phenomenological interviews (Seidman, 2006) are an ideal approach to gain an in-depth understanding of the university as a case, given the research questions on university people's experiences with national HE reform policies and with innovative practices.

A case, among other things, needs to be an object or entity, or an integrative or bounded system; a process or event fits the notion of a case less well. Miles and Huberman's (1994) depiction of a case is "a phenomenon of some sort occurring in a bounded context" (p. 25), and Merriam's (1998) interpretation is that a case needs to "graphically present itself as a circle with a heart in the center. The heart is the focus of the study, while the circle 'defines the edge of the case: what will not be studied'" (p. 27). A university serves as an ideal object in the classic sense of a case study, in it being a system with complex interacting factors with some edge separating it from its environment.

Other than having an ideal unit of analysis, this study on a university's responses to national policies and local innovations fits well other characteristics that R. Yin (2003) deems essential in distinguishing a case study from other types of studies such as survey, experimental or historical studies. In a case study, R. Yin states that "a 'how' or 'why' question is being asked about a contemporary set of events over which the investigator has little or no control" (p. 9). In other words, he maintains that a case study needs to meet the criteria in three areas, (a) the type of research questions should be "why" or "how", (b) the researcher has no control over the contexts and (c) the focus should be on contemporary issues.

First, in this research, I ask the questions how university people experience, reconstitute or resist national HE reform policies, and how they construct innovative practices. The purpose is to find as many in-depth details as possible. In Merriam's (1998) terms, this study provides "thick descriptions, is grounded, is holistic and lifelike, simplifies data to be considered by the reader, illuminates meanings, and can communicate tacit knowledge" (p. 39). The goal is not to "expand and generalize theories (analytic generalization) and not to enumerate frequencies (statistical generalization)" (R. Yin, 2003, p. 10). In other words, the research questions are designed to hold onto the meanings and vicarious details in the flood of happenings at the university, which separates the study from survey research.

Second, in this study, "the boundaries between phenomenon and context are not clearly evident" (R. Yin, 2003, p. 13), in that I have no control over the happenings in the university's environment. Unlike experimental studies that focus on a few variables in a controlled condition, this study examines the university of focus in its natural state, and I deliberately cover the contextual conditions in the belief that they are highly pertinent to the university I am studying. Third, this study pertains to contemporary issues—what is happening, current and ongoing.

In short, this study focuses on the university, the "bounded" system as a unit of analysis, and intends to find out the vicarious details, people's meaning interpretations of their lives under contextual conditions, such as national HE reform policies. This is a case study that meets with the characterizations across different literature (Merriam, 1998; Miles & Huberman, 1994; Stake, 1995).

Furthermore, the university of focus is a "typical" and "representative" case among many other universities in that it is a key university, a 211 and 985 grants recipient subject to the vagaries of national HE reform policies. Stake (1995) distinguishes *intrinsic* and *instrumental* case studies. Intrinsic cases are given to the researcher, for instance, a teacher is obliged to find out what is happening to a problematic student. The researcher is studying the case for its own sake and has no options over what cases to study. In instrumental cases, the cases are the means to some other issues, for instance, the university of focus is a vehicle through understanding national policy implementation or local innovations. The researcher has choices over a number of cases, and through a "typical" and "representative" case the researcher is able to find much more about the issues than through other cases. I will demonstrate in Chapter 3, the Methods section that, being a key university, and the recipient of major national unstipulated or block grants, and having a history of faithfully implementing national policies (such as reconstructing itself as a comprehensive university), the university of my choice is "typical" or "representative" according to Stake's and Merriam's (1998) standards.

There are no standardized protocols towards the data collection or data analysis in case studies, as Merriam (1998) states, "any and all methods of gathering data, from testing to interviewing, can be used in a case study" (p. 28, see also R. Yin, 2003). However, I will argue that some methodological tools are more appropriate than others in case studies, given the research questions. This case pertains to university people's sense making of their experiences of national HE reform policies and of innovative practices at the university of focus. Phenomenological interviews are an ideal tool in tapping the essence and structure of people's experiences. I will use Seidman's (2006) framework in conducting interviews in this case-study research. Furthermore, although triangulation of methods is recommended by most case-study theorists, or even used as a criterion to judge research validity (Miles & Huberman, 1994; R. Yin, 2003), Seidman maintains that phenomenological interviews do not necessarily combine with other methods, especially when the philosophical underpinnings—the assumptions of "what it means to understand the experience of others" (p. 6)—underlying different methods do not converge. This case-study research uses phenomenological interviews, which "when done with skill, can avoid tensions that sometimes arise when a researcher uses multiple methods" (p. 6). Detailed data collection and analysis process and the philosophical orientations underlying it will be further explained in Chapter 3, the Method section.

Overview of the Research

I will provide a brief overview of the chapters that follow this introductory chapter. The literature review in Chapter 2 is composed of two parts. The first part is a review of the *texts*, *contexts* and *consequences* of two national HE reform policies, amalgamation and expansion, through which one catches a glimpse of the official rationales and motivations, the "grand narratives" on HE reform. The second part of literature builds up a context for understanding national quality assurance mechanisms and how they filter all the way down to the university of focus and become institutionalized and operationalized in the way the university of focus chooses to measure faculty members' teaching and research performance. At the international level, there is a trend towards "audit culture" and "deprofessionalization" of academic professions. At the national level, strong mechanisms of teaching and research quality assurance exist, with the "performance indicators" bear subtle economic and political agenda. In short, both parts of literature review explains the background of national HE reform policies, amalgamation, expansion and quality assurance mechanisms; it is vis-à-vis these macro-policies, that university people's perceptions and responses are assessed and illustrated in Chapters 4 and 5.

In Chapter 3 I will detail the concrete process in which the phenomenological interviews are conducted: How is the setting selected? How are interview participants drawn, and data collected and analyzed? Throughout the chapter, I make the philosophical and theoretical assumptions underlying each step of the process explicit, given that phenomenological interviews are unique and need to be justified in the eyes of those who are used to "triangulation" of data sources.

Chapters 4 to 6 will be analyses on the interviews of the university of focus, each corresponds to a research question posed in the introductory chapter. Chapter 4 will be on the university people's perceptions of and reactions to the expansion and amalgamation policies. In Chapter 5, I will analyze two layers of impacts of national quality assurance mechanisms on the university people: a direct impact, and an impact through co-opting the university's internal mechanisms, such as the teaching supervising (*dudao*) team, and faculty promotion criteria. Both Chapters 4 and 5 suggest that there is a high-level of "political reflexivity" and resistance among frontline faculty members, administrators and students towards national HE reform policies: amalgamation, expansion and quality assurance mechanisms. There is an "implementation gap" between national HE reform policies and their "situated practices" at the university of focus.

In Chapter 6, I will use a "grounded" approach to examine the local innovations at the university of focus. Instead of constructing preconceived conceptions of innovations, I inductively describe what innovations are in the perspectives of administrators, faculty members and students. These innovations are grounded in local people's meaning-making systems and in harmony with their perceptions of the organizational purposes, and therefore, embodiment of genuine changes, unlike the official accounts of HE reform.

In the last chapter, Chapter 7, I will discuss the lessons learned from this phenomenological case study. First, I will summarize the findings in the previous chapters. Second, I will stress the importance of distinguishing universities, which naturally defy top-down, centralized reform efforts, from other models of organizations (such as business organizations and annexations of governmental bureaus). Bottom-up and inside-out reforms are more appropriate for universities. Third, I will propose an alternative to the top-down, centralized policymaking, with attendant attention to policy analysts' role in the alternative model.

Chapter 2
Literature Review

This literature review chapter provides background information on the national HE reform policies that are examined in this case-study research: amalgamation, expansion and national quality assurance mechanisms. In the first part of the literature review, I introduce the *contexts*, *texts* and *consequences* of two national HE reform policies, amalgamation and expansion. In the second part of the literature review on national quality assurance mechanisms, as the accountability movements or the rise of "audit culture" is a prevailing and ongoing phenomenon across most HE systems in the world (Shore & Wright, 1999, 2000; Trow, 1994, 1996a; Dill, 1997; Morley, 2002, 2003; Brennan & Shah, 2000a, 2000b), I follow the trajectory of "policy dynamics from global contexts, through the national level to policy reconstruction and practices within institutions at the micro level" (Vidovich et al., 2007, p. 93). In this second part of literature review, I discuss the rise of "audit culture" and "deprofessionalization" of academic professions in the international arena. Then, I proceed to explain the teaching and research quality assurance mechanisms at Chinese national level.

The literature review chapter provides background information on the national HE reform policies and should be read vis-à-vis the analysis of the lived experiences of academics, administrators and students in Chapters 4 and 5. As I use a "grounded", inductive-deductive approach to examine another topic of this research, the innovations at the university level, I did not do a literature review on that topic. So Chapter 6 stands by itself.

Amalgamation and Expansion

The amalgamation of universities started off around 1992 and continued into late 2006, which according to Mohrman's (2003) observation is co-opting all Chinese universities despite their complacency or reluctance. The "reactive growth" (Clark, 1996) of universities—the expansion of undergraduate enrolments, broaching in the year of 1999, was deemed "a Great Leap Forward" in HE development history, and was followed by a prospect of graduate enrolments expansion in 2008. This research chooses to evaluate these two policies. In the first place, both policies have profound and lasting impacts on the landscape of HE today. In the second place, both policies last around 10 years or more. Gamage (1992) suggests that it is futile to evaluate short-lived policies; it takes a long time for some policies to take effect, such as the efficiency gains through the amalgamation policy.

As I have explained in the Introduction, national HE reform policies are neoliberal-ideology driven; the concern for efficiency and effective coordination of scarce resources, and universities as engines of the national economy, has dominated the HE reform policy discourses since 1993, to a degree that other competing values are rendered nominal. And the policy processes are highly centralized. In the first part of Chapter 2, I will illustrate the "efficiency/economy is good" mentality in the top-down policymaking, through analyzing the *contexts*, *texts* and *consequences* of amalgamation and expansion, which is an analytic framework suggested by Tatkirm, Rizvi, Lingard and Henry (1997; see also Bell & Stevenson, 2006).

Contexts, texts and consequences of policies

According to Tatkirm et al. (1997), and Bell and Stevenson (2006), policy is not only a product, but a process. Policy involves the introduction of the policy contexts, the texts themselves, the ongoing modification to the texts, and the process of implementation into practice. Thus I not only focus on analyzing documents/texts, but also follow the ongoing policy process, from a policy's historical precedents, social-economic factors that lead to its generation all the way to the aftermath of its implementation.

Contexts. The analysis of contexts includes three overlapping aspects. First, the historical contexts, the previous development of other cognate policies, as policies are likely to be incremental and "intertextual." They seldom come all of a sudden out of a vacuum, but are related to antecedents and the historical conditions created by those antecedents (Darling-Hammond, 1990). Second, more contemporary domestic contexts like the economic, social, political factors which lead to an issue being placed upon the policy agenda. Third, international conditions, such as policy borrowing from countries facing similar problems (Green, 1997, 1999) and policy covenants attached to treaties/contracts with international organizations (Ginsburg, Cooper, Raghu, & Zegarra, 1990; Jones, 2007; McNeely, 1995; McNeely & Cha, 1994). It is more difficult to establish the direct casual relationships between this set of influences on education, as they are more general, remote and sometimes deliberately concealed. International contexts for amalgamation and expansion are only inferential and suggestive.

Texts. I use sources like governmental policy documents, elite journal articles, media release, governmental year books, public speeches by officials from educational bureaus—the elements of what Fox and Fox (2004) term as "corporate public discourse"—as the texts of policies.

Consequences. I am using empirical evidence (e. g. empirical studies in journal articles) to evaluate the realized consequences of amalgamation and expansion, despite the rarity of this type of materials. My focus is on the contrast between the consequences as perceived (e. g. policy goals) and consequences as realized.

Amalgamation

Amalgamation is defined as "the combination of two or more separate organizations into a single entity, with overall management control being under a single governing body and a single chief executive" (Harman, 2000; see also Gamage, 1992,1993). The amalgamation or merger of Chinese universities and colleges comes in many forms. For the purpose of this discussion, two distinctions are made. First, a distinction between consolidation and acquisition. In the former case, two or more institutions of equal strength merge without significantly affecting the structure of each, while in the latter case, the weaker institution(s) is likely to be absorbed or dissolve into the stronger, master institution. Second, the distinction between horizontal and vertical amalgamations. The former denotes the merger of two or more institutions specializing in teaching and research in parallel areas (e. g., two comprehensive universities) whereas the latter of institutions in different areas (e. g., a technological college and a medical college).

Contexts of amalgamation. One historical condition for amalgamation was set forth by the 1952—1957 HE reform (M. A. Xiong, 1995; Q. Zhang & Pang, 2004) after the establishment of the People's Republic of China, a period that Hartnett (1996) terms as "mindless copying" of the former Soviet Union (see also R. Yang, 2002). In that period, the nascent country was in need of harnessing HE for the burgeoning socialist economy, with the most immediate need being cultivating a labor force for the first five-year plan of industrial construction (D. Y. Chen, 2002). The higher education system handed down from the Nationalist Era (1927—1945) was unsatisfactorily liberal arts/social sciences oriented (e. g. , law and politics), with only 31% enrolments in science and technological areas (e. g. animal husbandry, agriculture, engineering) (Hartnett, 1996). So the guiding principles for the 1952—1957 restructuring were "cultivating a workforce for industrial development and education, and developing specialized institutions" (Q. Zhang & Pang, p. 81; see also M. A. Xiong, 1995).

Under the framework of maximizing the output of specialized high-level human resources (the "red and expert" talents, such as teachers, technicians, and agricultural, health, and art specialists), two important initiatives were made among many others. First, some technological departments/units were disintegrated from the multi-purpose universities and became independent, individualized institutions. Second, many new specialized technological institutes were established under the jurisdiction of each governmental Ministry in the central or local government (e. g. , Ministry of Finance, Ministry of Medicine, Ministry of Agricultural). They were dispersed in the locales where the economy needed them most. This created a fragmented system of narrowly-specialized, small-scale, and low-enrolment institutions. For instance, in 1988, 56.2% of 1,075 institutions had an enrolment of lower than 1,500 students whereas only 6.6% had an enrolment of over 5,000 students (F. Zhao, 1998).

In the 30 years since the economic liberation in 1978, the HE system was constantly accused of low efficiency and effectiveness, failing to serve the economic, social, and cultural needs of the rapidly developing society (Mok, 2005a). Institutional merger was trusted into the central position of solving educational and economic problems.

In the first place, university merger is expected to improve *internal efficiency*. It is proposed that a small institution with small student-teacher ratio (STR) can significantly increase its enrolments with proportionately less increase in its resources. In other words, a larger institution has lower unit costs (per student expenditure) than a small one. This theory is alternatively called economy of scale, although researchers caution that when the scale exceeds certain threshold standard, the economy of scale turns into diseconomy (X. H. Ding & Min, 1997; Min & X. H. Ding, 1993; Tsang & Min, 1992). In 1986, a World Bank mission report, based on data obtained from 136 universities, convincingly concluded that an enrolment of 8,000—10,000 would be optimal for economy of scale at Chinese universities, while smaller or larger size might induce larger unit costs (World Bank, 1986). Thus it is proposed that small institutions in adjacent areas might consider amalgamation.

In the second place, *external* efficiency is defined by an HE institution's breath of curricula. It is hypothesized that a student experiencing a wider range of curricula in universities is more able to learn new knowledge and adaptable to the variations in the workplaces and society (X. H. Ding & Min, 1997; Gamage, 1992, 1993; Harman, 2000; Min & X. H. Ding, 1993; Tsang & Min, 1992). This argument fits into a broader conceptual framework of lifelong learning or learning society (Harman, 2000). In short, amalgamation is expected to improve external efficiency of universities.

Besides striving for economic efficiency, university amalgamation is more directly motivated by the 211 Project (and later 985 Project), a governmental effort to develop around 100 top universities for the 21st century (MoE, 2004a), which disburses generous funding to support universities with the potential to achieve the "world-class" status. World-class universities are narrowly seen as achievable through monetary investments and building large-scale infrastructure in the image of Kerr's (1972) conceptualization of "multiversity" or "aircraft carrier" (L. Zhou, 2000a, 2000b). University magnitude, or the range of disciplines a university harbors, is a prerequisite of disbursing 211 Project funding. One "quick-fix" step towards attracting 211 funding is combining existing flagship universities. For instance, acquiring specialized medical colleges becomes a trendy strategy for comprehensive universities to further develop "comprehensiveness" (D. Y. Chen, 2002).

Some observers view the tidal wave as voluntary, market-driven and self-directed by universities striving for efficiency and effectiveness in a neoliberal market. For instance, R. Yang (2002), comparing it with the 1952—1957 reform, concludes that the current reform is bottom-up, comparatively more adaptable to local needs and has no definite timeline. Y. M. Wan's (2008) case study of the merger of Zhejiang University attributes the merger initiative to the university leaders' aspirations. "The future they envisioned for their institutions and the merger plan they had brewed in their mind turned out to chime well with the government agenda" (p. 179).

More observers, however, have maintained that it is the governmental power of purse that triggers the tidal wave of amalgamation (G. J. Gao, 2001; Yuan & Jiang, 2000; P. J. Wang, 1996). Drawing on resource dependence theory (Slaughter & Leslie, 1997), they maintain that, rather than mandate amalgamation directly, the government "steers at a distance," making amalgamation an implicit condition for disbursing 211 Project funding, which makes non-compliance not an option. Furthermore, university leaders, instead of being autonomous actors, usually obtain sanctions, or at least acquiescence from governmental authorities before making decisions and taking actions. They are "acting in accordance to upper-level 'red' papers (*hongtou wenjian*); or they report everything to higher-level authorities, taking actions only after having obtained governmental sanctions," comments G. J. Gao (2001, p. 10; see also Mohrman, 2003). What appears as campus-level autonomous decisions and peer effects among universities bears the imprint of governmental will and intensions.

There is only inferential evidence on the international context for university amalgamation in China. Amalgamation is trendy in a neoliberal ideological context where universities are governed along the lines of efficiency, corporatism and managerialism (Mok, 2005a). Rich literature documents the amalgamation in Australia, Japan, US, South Africa, and multiple European countries (Gamage, 1992, 1993; Goedegebuure, 1992; Harman, 2000; R. Y. Xie, 2004; Y. M. Wan, 2008; Y. M. Wan & Peterson, 2007), all as responses to problems such as diminishing financial support, shrinking high-school graduate pool, and the need for improving effectiveness and efficiency. According to Hayhoe (1996), in 1992, the World Bank as a covenant of its educational loans to China, "encouraged the amalgamation of small and often specialized local colleges into larger and more comprehensive higher institutions" (pp. 135 – 136).

Texts of amalgamation. A number of policy texts contributed to the trend towards amalgamation. In May, 1985, the central government issued *Decisions On the Reforms of Educational System* (MoE, 1985) at its congressional meeting, which emphasized "reform, expansion and cooperation" rather than establishing new institutions as the guiding principles of higher education reform. This led to some sporadic, experimental cases of mergers. Stronger voices for amalgamation came around in the period of 1993—1995. The then Prime Minister, Li Peng (1995), in a variety of public speeches, emphasized that jointly-run institutions including consolidation and cooperation of institutions might optimize educational resources.

The then Minister of Education, Zhu Kaixuan (1995) followed Li Peng, proposing that conditions needed be created to promote consolidation of those small institutions with a narrow range of specialties and redundant courses; and that those specialized institutions in adjacent areas be encouraged to set up cooperative relations and share resources. He said that

> It is difficult to solve the problem of shortage of finance in a short run. To solve the shortage, apart from relying on governmental input, each institution should seek to reform and restructure, to optimize the distribution of resources, that is, to maximize usage of limited resources…. We need to build more comprehensive, large institutions. Most world-renowned universities are large and comprehensive, which is conducive to the cultivation of talents and harboring breakthrough in research. In our univertsity system, small specialized institutions are the mainstream. It is impossible and unnecessary to develop these institutions into large comprehensive ones. Our only realistic choice is to restructure these institutions, and concentrate the resources on some comprehensive universities… (p.2)

The pinnacle of amalgamation, however, was created by the vice Prime Minister, Li Lanqing's 2000 speech *A Report On The Strategy Of Revitalizing The Nation Through Science and Technology*, in which he not only reiterated the slogan "gongjian, tiaozhen, hezuo, hebing" (co-investing, restructuring, cooperation and amalgamation), but also promulgated specific guidelines on conducting amalgamation. His speech went that

> The HE system in our country should provide high-

quality interdisciplinary talents for the development of the economy...we need to change that universities are run by the ministries, are narrowly specialized and focusing on a small range of disciplines, and the resources are dispersed. We need to re-coordinate the resources so as to improve quality and efficiency. Having experimented in a small scale, we need to accelerate the HE reform under the guidance of "co-investing, restructuring, cooperation and amalgamation".... This year, 612 HE institutions have merged into 250 institutions...The institutions enhance their disciplinary strengths and build university zones where labs and faculty members are shared and students are taking courses and earning credits across multiple institutions. In addition, these institutions share joint logistic systems. We have realized, to some humble extent, the optimal coordination of resources in which the strength and weakness of different institutions are complemented.

Hereby, he set in motion the 15-year amalgamation, during which 875 institutions (adult education excluded) were merged into 363 (for major amalgamations, please refer to Table 1).

Table 1　Major Cases of University Mergers

University	Institutions Merged
Beijing University	Beijing University, Beijing University of Medical Sciences
Tsinghua University	Tsinghua University, Central Academy of Techniques Arts
Nankai University	Nankai University, Tianjin College of Foreign Trade
Northeastern University	Northeastern University, Gold College
Jilin University	Jilin University, Jilin Industry University, Baiqiuen University of Medical Sciences, Changchun University of Science and Technology, Changchun College of Postal and Communication

续表

University	Institutions Merged
Fudan University	Fudan University, Shanghai University of Medical Sciences
Tongji University	Tongji University, Shanghai Railway University, Shanghai College of City Construction, Shanghai College of Construction Materials
Shanghai Jiaotong University	Shanghai Jiaotong University, Shanghai Agriculture College
Huadong University of Science and Technology	Huadong University of Science and Technology, Jinshan Petrochemical College
Donghua University	China Textile University, Shanghai Textile College
East-China Teacher's University	East-China Teacher's University, Shanghai College of Ed., Shanghai No.2 College of Education, Shanghai Teacher's College for Children
Southeast University	Southeast University, Nanjing College of Railway Medical Sciences, Nanjing Jiaotong College
Zhejiang University	Zhejiang University, Hangzhou University, Zhejiang University of Medical Sciences, Zhejiang Agriculture University
Shandong University	Shandong University, Shandong University of Medical Sciences, Shandong Industry University
Wuhan University	Wuhan University, Wuhan University of Hydroelectric, Wuhan University of Mapping and Survey, Hubei University of Medical Sciences
Huazhong University of Science and Technology	Huazhong University of Science and Technology, Tongji University of Medical Sciences, Wuhan College of City Construction, Wuhan Training College of Science and Technology for Cadres
Hunan University	Hunan University, Hunan University of Finance

Note: Adapted from "The amalgamation of Chinese higher education institutions" by D. Y. Chen, 2002, *Education Policy Analysis Archives*, 10(20).

The diagram for the number of cases of amalgamation by year (see Table 2) looks roughly like a bell-shaped curve, with its two tails stretching towards early 90s and 2006, and its peak at 2000 when 96 cases of amalgamation occurred.

Table 2 Instances of University Merger by Year (Ends as on May 15, 2006)

Year	Instances of university merger
1992	11
1993	9
1994	8
1995	21
1996	15
1997	17
1998	26
1999	30
2000	96
2001	39
2002	42
2003	22
2004	15
2005	9
2006	3

Note: Adapted from "The amalgmation of universities since 1990" by MoE (2006b). Retrieved September 7, 2009 from http://www.moe.edu.cn/edoas/website18/18/info3318.htm

Consequences of amalgamation. Meek's (1988) comments on the nation-wide university amalgamation in Australia expressed a rather sanguine view, stating that people tend to assess the mergers positively in retrospect. The benefits of Chinese amalgamation between 1992 and 2006, are inconclusive on the basis of existing empirical studies, perhaps because, as Gamage (1992) maintains that economy of scale can only be achieved in a long-, but not short-run. Despite the rarity and fragmentation of existing empirical studies on the outcomes of amalgamation, I am assessing the consequences of amalgamation in three terms, as is a modified version of Harman's (2000) framework for evaluating post-merger integration of universities: efficiency gains or losses; impact on academic programs and services; future organizational stability.

Efficiency gains and losses. Student-teacher ratio (STR) and student-staff ratio (SSR) are two indicators frequently applied to assess the efficiency of post-amalgamation universities. As I have argued before, the pre-amalgamation systems are typically characterized by low student-faculty/staff ratio, low enrolments and high unit costs (Min, 1991). Min calculated in 1991 that the average STR in China was 5.2, as compared to 15.2 in all Asian countries, and 10 to 15 in Western developed countries. The SSR was 2.1, even strikingly lower. Significant improvement of STR indicator is reported in university merger cases, due to a slight attrition of faculty members during the merger, and rapid expansion of enrolments. For instance, rapid improvement of STR, from 7.85 to 11.08 in three years, was witnessed in the merger of Fudan and Shanghai Medical College (L. Xu, 2003). However, as the two major reform policies, amalgamation and expansion were enmeshed with each other, it was difficult to determine whether increased STR was solely a function of amalgamation.

The improvement of SSR, however, was less obvious due to a variety of factors. Y. M. Wan (2008) indicates that university mergers occurred by combining parallel units of different institutions. Although downsizing was integral to merger, for instance, the New Zhejiang University reduced its administrator positions from 1,000 to 800 and further to 600 during its amalgamation process, redundant administrators/staff were demoted/ repositioned rather than laid off. Similarly, W. Pan (2004) finds a proliferation rather than retrenchment of administrative/service units in post-amalgamation institutions. The competing units insist on different organizational procedures, making it increasingly difficult to get things done (see also G. Y. Guo, 1998). L. Xu (2003) finds that, as Fudan and Shanghai medical college campuses are far apart, all existing administration/service units on each campus remained intact after the amalgamation, whereas a significant number of staff positions have to be created to facilitate the communication between two campuses. That is, administrative costs significantly rise but do not reduce after amalgamation. Furthermore, unexpected costs, such as commutation between different campuses, professional development for unqualified personnel, raising salaries might incur to the amalgamated institutions. For instance, Jilin University, after acquiring other five small institutions, was involved in a debt of ¥30 billion in 2007, partly because it had to raise salaries of all acquired institutions to a rate that matched the original Jilin University (H. W. Ma, 2007).

In short, the analysis of efficiency gains and losses indicates that it would be naive and optimistic to conceive of amalgamation as a panacea for efficiency and cost reduction. At least in the short run, economy of scale remains a myth rather than a reality.

Impact on academic programs and services. There are scarce empirical data supporting how students gain from a multiplicity of disciplines on campus. In cases of acquisition merger, there is significant improvement of student and faculty quality and increase of governmental funding (G. Y. Guo, 1998; L. Xu, 2003). This might be indirect proof of the improvement of the quality of academic programs and services. For instance, students are admitted according to the standards of the master flagship universities, which are significantly higher than pre-amalgamation institutions. Academics from smaller, less-prestigious institutions are coerced to receive professional development training and periodical performance assessments (Y. M. Wan, 2008) to match the expectation of the flagship universities. So overall, there is improvement in faculty academic ranks as well as research outputs. For instance, the ratio of full professors and associate professors to all faculty members increased from 58.6% to 63.6% in three years after Fudan merger (L. Xu, 2003). Furthermore, amalgamated universities are more likely to have new doctoral or master programs accredited, so as to become more research based. For instance, Guangdong University of Technology, developed its first doctoral program, and added 10 to 3 Master's programs in five years after amalgamation. Despite their rarity, existing data do point to the positive outcomes for teaching and research after merger.

Future organizational stability. The future stability of organization is held in constant question in university merger literature, as current amalgamation is based on the principle of economic efficiency; strategic deployment of economic resources neglects the nature of academic culture that is notoriously self-directed, bottom-heavy and resistant to external impositions (Trowler, 2001, 2002, 2005; Weick, 1976). In a Chinese university amalgamation, the agreement usually was reached between governmental officials and university leaders instead of grounded in the general acceptance of ordinary faculty members, staffs and students (Y. M. Wan, 2008). Furthermore, amalgamation decision was generally made on the basis of economic efficiency, such as the geographical locations of different campuses, complementarity between disciplines, but not cultural compatibility, which might turn out to be a source of resistance or at least impediment to post-merger integration (J. Wang, 2007; Q. Wang & J. Lin, 2005).

The existing literature suggests that merger at physical, or organizational procedural levels are more easily achieved than at cultural level; each institution, in its decades of separate development, has developed a unique system of beliefs, attitudes, values, symbols and rituals that are perceived as true by its members (J. Wang, 2007; Y. M. Wan, 2008). Faculty and staff resistance is defined as the utmost impediment to successful post-merger integration, although it is less obvious in mergers based on "common history." For instance, Sichuan University and Chengdu Institute of Science and Technology were disintegrated in the 1952—1957 HE reform from the old Sichuan University; the year of 1994 witnessed the reunification of the two institutions, physically separated only by one street. Zhejiang University has acquired three other institutions that originally were part of it before 1952. Such "common history" was stressed during the amalgamation process and was generally accepted by people (Y. M. Wan & Peterson, 2007).

In other types of mergers, there are strong faculty and staff dissatisfaction and attrition of employees. For instance, a survey conducted at Nanjing University of Finance indicates that 60% of faculty members and staffs find there is a deterioration of interpersonal relationship (J. Wang, 2007). Q. Wang and J. Lin's (2005) survey on four post-amalgamation universities in Shanxi and Shaanxi suggests that most faculty members are not satisfied with the post-merger environment despite the improvement in personal incomes, well-being, personal and professional development opportunities. Partly it is attributed to the proliferation of administrative units after merger. More administrative units are in charge of teaching and research so that faculty members have even less discretion in their professional work.

Besides low satisfaction rate with jobs, the old boundaries of different institutions psychologically linger in people's mind, despite the announcement of their disappearance. For instance, Y. M. Wan's (2008) study finds out that students at former Zhejiang University refuse to be relocated on the campus of the former Zhejiang Agricultural University, despite the fact that the two universities have amalgamated. Their fear is that being physically located on the campus of a less prestigious college before amalgamation will tarnish their academic credentials and isolate them from the "mainstream" master university. Either faculty members, administrators and students, or people outside of the universities, continue to use universities' original names to identify and separate the different campuses. All such evidence suggests that, despite the governmental and administrative fiats and the "thunderbolt" efforts in unifying the organizational units and procedures, there are areas that cannot be reached by administrative coercion, which poses a threat to the hypothesized success of merger.

Expansion.

Contexts of Expansion. There are multiple factors that gave rise to the undergraduate expansion policy, the "Great Leap Forward" in Chinese HE in June, 1999. One of the driving factors is the chronicle low enrolment rate, the acute tensions between the demand and supply of HE. Table 3 compares the gross enrolment rate of China (from 1999 to 2007) with other Asian and Western developed countries. However, what finally gave birth to the expansion policy in 1999, is not the motive to improve enrolments, but the concern for economic gains, as undergraduate expansion is constantly calibrated for its internal and external relation to national economic development.

Table 3 Comparing Enrolment Rate to East Asian/Pacific and Western Developed Countries

Countries	Gross Enrolment Rate								
	'99	'00	'01	'02	'03	'04	'05	'06	'07
China	6	8	10	13	16	18	20	22	23
Japan	45	47	49	51	52	54	55	57	58
Korea	73	78	83	87	89	90	91	93	73
Singapore	...	...	...	...	...	...	...	...	...
Australia	65	66	67	76	74	72	73	73	75

续表

Countries	Gross Enrolment Rate								
	'99	'00	'01	'02	'03	'04	'05	'06	'07
France	52	53	54	53	55	56	56	56	56
Germany	...	...	...	...	...	...	...	...	...
UK	60	58	59	63	63	60	59	59	59
Canada	60	59	...	60	...	(**) 62	...	...	...
US	73	69	70	80	82	82	82	82	82

Note: Adapted from "Key statistic tables: Table 14 tertiary indicators" by UNESCO Institute for Statistics [UIS].

... means that data are not available.

(**) means UIS estimation.

  Chinese HE is characterized by low enrolment rate. According to R. J. Wang (2003), the rate of college students as percentage of the total population was 0.28 in 1999, lower by 10 times than any of the "economic miracles" such as Japan, Korea, (with an exception of Singapore) and developed countries in Northern America and Western Europe such as the United States, Canada and the United Kingdom. As Table 3 indicates, the gross enrolment rate (the ratio of college enrolments to the college-age cohort in the population) was only 6% in 1999, lower by 8 to 12 times than developed countries. Even after around eight years of substantial expansion from 1999 to 2006, and after having reached the threshold rate of 15% for mass HE in 2003 (Trow, 1973), the gross enrolment rate is still lower than these developed countries by 2 or 3 times. This fact indicates that low enrolment rate and the tension between HE demand and supply is a factor in the "Great Leap Forward" in the year of 1999.

  What finally gave rise to the expansion policy in June, 1999 was the concern for economic values of HE. Traditionally, economic values of HE are discussed in terms of human-resource theory, the way that HE helps to develop skills and improve the economic capabilities of people. Such human abilities, fixed in persons, contribute to the national economic growth like tangible capitals (e. g., land and equipment) (Kang, 2000; Sweetland, 1996; K. Y. Xie, 2003). The motivation behind the 1999 expansion policy, however, centers on HE's contribution to GDP through student tuitions, living expenditures, and investments on campus facilities. For instance, many scholars have attributed the expansion policy to Tang and Zuo's (1999a, 1999b) research work, in which they make crude estimation that in three years, if the undergraduate enrolments increase by 2 million, students' tuitions would mount to 200 billion, and their living expenditures 40 billion. Furthermore, the process of expansion (such as building construction) provided job opportunities for relevant industries and services (X. H. Ding & L. K. Chen, 2000), which would contribute to the GDP by 1,000 billion. In total, the revenues from expanded enrolments account for 0.5% of national GDP. Tang and Zuo further argue that HE, like a reservoir, would retain 2 million high-school graduates from directly entering the labor market, and substantially alleviate the escalating unemployment rate (albeit temporarily) caused by the Asian Economic Recession in 1997. They argue that

> The high school graduates are competing for jobs with laid-off workers ... If we are sending them to universities, they will make places for the laid-off workers. After four years, we have solved the problem of Asian economic recession... it might be easier to provide jobs for these same persons who are now university graduates. It is said that the military draft in Korea serves the same purpose as to alleviate the pressure of unemployment. Turning high school graduates into university students is certainly wiser than turning them

into soldiers. (1999a, p. 1)

Similar conclusions are espoused by multiple other economists (K. F. Gu, 2006; Kang, 2000; Su, 2000). Research Team at Beijing University (2001) follows this line of calculation, albeit claiming to be more accurate and seeking ways to maximize income from HE expansion. The research suggests that the bulk of revenues created through expansion would not be tuitions and students' living expenses, but through building new facilities and infrastructure to accommodate those students, which is extrapolated to contribute to annual GDP by 322 billion. The authors further propose to maximize tuition revenue through a "double-track" admission policy. In the model the authors build, if high-score students are to pay the normal tuition (e.g., ¥3,000) while low-score students are made to pay more (e.g., ¥11,020) to compensate for their inadequacy in scores, the tuition revenue would increase by 72% compared to undifferentiated admission policy.

All these calculations on the hypothetical revenue from HE expansion are expected to be realized, as a plethora of research points to Chinese parents' exceptional willingness to save and disburse for their children's HE, especially when the first-generation of the only child is coming of age (Research Team at Beijing University, 2001; Hawkins, 2000). For instance, according to Lai's (2004) survey, 91.9% of city dwellers hope that their children will own undergraduate degrees or higher. In 2004, the total family savings were estimated to be 11,000,000 billion Yuan, a great proportion of which are savings for children's education. This indicates that Chinese parents are not only willing but also able to pay for their children's college tuitions.

In short, it is the concern for the economic values of HE that motivated the undergraduate expansion policy between 1999 and 2006, as Yan and Chang (2008) comment rather bitterly that "expansion is centered on creating economic opportunities … the government uses people's earnest quest for HE, as a means to boost the economy" (p.45; see also H. C. Wang, 2004). The policy is based on "government's subjective intension ... aims to realize government's strategic plan to a maximum degree" (Lin, 2007, p. 61). Although the dust of undergraduate expansion had settled down in 2006, the heated discussions on graduate expansion arouse, again vested with the hope of absorbing unemployed undergraduates and boosting the sluggish economy in 2008 (Yan & Chang, 2008).

The expansion policy in China is not directly attributable to an international context. However, it is situated in a condition that the World Bank is shifting its subsidiaries from elementary and secondary to tertiary education in developing countries (Jones, 2007). It is reasoned that, as a skilled work force commands a premium in the transition from a manufacture- to knowledge-centered society, resources should be redirected from lower-level to tertiary education. Without substantial expansion and development of their university systems, developing countries might be risking exclusion in the knowledge economy (Task Force on Higher Education and Society, 2000).

Texts of expansion. There are documents and texts that record the inception, implementation and termination of undergraduate expansion, all emanating from the national center, MoE. I will select three major benchmark texts that indicate the punctuated points in the expansion process. First, at the Third National Congressional Meeting on Education, in June 1999, three public speeches by top political leaders Jiang Zheming (1999) and Zhu Rongji (1999) simultaneously referred to university expansion as one of the goals to be achieved, which is regarded as the formal inception of university expansion. It was reiterated that "the nation should expand the current scope of university and adult education, to meet people's needs for HE to a maximum degree. Meanwhile, social resources should be mobilized to establish people-run institutions, as a supplement to the current HE system" (Jiang, 1999). Zhu Rongji's speech at the closing ceremony was recognized as the official inception of the expansion policy. Zhu said that

> It is important and impending to accelerate the development of education. Currently, the labor force in our country is not well educated, and education is a much sought-after resource by both city and rural dwellers. Through enhancing educational development, we can achieve multiple goals such as quenching the thirst for education, focusing on quality education, and elevating the quality of the citizenry... Furthermore, expanding education can stimulate citizens' spending on education and boost the economy...The city and rural dwellers not only have strong desires for education, but also have savings that could be spent on it. We have untapped resources and can further mobilize investments from the society.

As Song and Liao (2004) state that "in our country, public speeches by political leaders indicate governmental sanctions of certain policy initiatives" (p. 26), these speeches heralded an age of substantial and aggressive university expansion between 1999 and 2006.

Second, more detailed goals on expansion were stipulated in two successive governmental documents, *Action Plan on Revitalizing Education for 21st Century* (MoE, 1998), and *The Tenth Five-year Plan On Education* (MoE, 2002). In the former 1998 document, the MoE set more moderate goals as to raise gross enrolments to 11% by the year of 2000. It stipulateed that

> In order that more high school graduates can enter HE institutions... HE enrolments can be raised to 660

million...The gross rate can be improved from 9.1% in 1997 to 11% in 2000. The student and teacher ratio can be changed from 10:1 to 12:1. An independent, average HE institution may have a student body of 4,000. (MoE, 1998)

However, as the gross enrolment rate already surpassed 15% in 2002, the MoE (2002) revised its goals, stipulating that gross enrolments should hit 20% in 2010.

The total new enrolments in all types of HE institutions reached 23 million, including 1 million graduate students. The gross enrolment rate is expected to reach 20%. We should further enhance the innovative and service capacities of HE institutions, and further deepen reforms on education and teaching... We should realize the basic modernization of education in some areas, and optimize the structure and distribution of HE institutions in a national scale.

As Yan and Chang (2008) comment, MoE made major revisions on expansion plan in a short time frame, which somehow indicates that expansion policy is unbridled and insufficiently planned, or even chaotic.

In December, 2003, when interviewed by *Zhongguo Qingnian Bao* (*Chinese Youth Daily*), the vice Prime Minister Li Lanqing looked in retrospect the decision on undergraduate expansion. He gave a relative comprehensive view on the four conditions that gave rise to this large-scale policy, indicating that the government was adamant about its enforcement. He said that

The decision on the large-scale undergraduate enrolment expansion, was made in early June, 1999 by Prime Minister Zhu Rongji... There are four rationales behind this policy. First is that the economic development in our country is demanding more high-quality talents... In terms of the ratio between university enrolments and the total population, we lag far behind not only developed countries but India...

Second, our citizens want their children to be college-educated, a desire that the government is obliged to cater to...

Third, the expansion of university enrolments prevents high school graduates from entering the labor market in an early stage. It increases the revenues from education, boosts the economy through stimulating spending and enhances the development of education-related industries.

Fourth, as in the past, university admissions were so limited that our education was focusing on passing the entrance examination. It is impossible to enforce quality-education in a large scale.

Therefore, the expansion policy is unavoidable and converges with the Chinese people's will. The facts prove that this is a right decision. (L. Q. Li, 2003)

Third, in May 2006, at the regular congressional meeting convened by the Prime Minister Wen Jiabao, it was stipulated that it was essential to curtail university expansion, given the current conditions of the university system. He said that

We have achieved tremendously in HE development and reform. In 2005, we admitted 5.04 million university students, a 4.7-time increase than in 1998; the gross enrolment rate has reach 21%, and the total university student enrolments are 23 million, making the university system the largest in the world. We have achieved mass education. Our HE has cultivated a large number of high-quality talents for the modernization and contributes tremendously to the development of the society and economy. However, we should not deny the other side of the problem, that there are many challenges and pitfalls in the current HE system. Especially, the quality of HE does not match the development of the economy and society. There are large spaces for improvement with regard to educational philosophy, methodologies, and content and methods of teaching. The quality of faculty members needs to be further improved. We did not invest sufficiently in HE, so that some institutions are lacking in resources. University graduates face unemployment problems. (MoE, 2006a)

He further stipulated that it is more important to improve the quality than expanding enrolments. Wen's speech is regarded as the official conclusion of expansion policy, after which the growth in enrolments is restricted to 5% or lower each year.

Consequences of expansion. The undergraduate enrolments policy has created a spectacular and grandiose picture of HE change. Between 1998 and 2006, undergraduate enrolments had increased by 5 to 6 times, with each year's increase ranging between 20% to 50%. By the year of 2004, China had the largest university system in terms of students' number in the world. The detailed statistics on annual enrolment and gross enrolment rates between 1999 and 2006 can be found in J. Li (2009), Zha (2009) and F. L. Li, Morgan and X. H. Ding (2008). However, as a centralized, top-down policy that in a simplistic and reductionist way stresses HE as part of national economic mechanism, the expansion policy is controversial as well. I will discuss the social justice, quality, and graduate unemployment issues as consequences of implementation of undergraduate expansion.

Social justice. An integral part of expansion policy is students' cost-sharing, as part of anticipated revenue of expansion comes from increased students' tuitions (Tang & Zuo, 1999a; Research Team at Beijing University, 2001; W. L. Li, 2002; J. F. Li & P. Guo, 2004). This fact has divergent implications for low- and high-social economic status (SES) students. W. L. Li builds a statistic model, which indicates that as tuitions increase by 1%, 0.562% of families/individuals will refrain from choosing HE. Furthermore, low-income families/individuals are twice as sensitive to the fluctuation of tuitions. In other words, low-income families/individuals are twice likely to withdraw from education as their high-income counterparts as tuitions increase. Given the vast disparity in income level between urban and rural areas in China, Kang (2000) and M. Zhou (2007) find stark contrastive reactions to the expansion policy among urban and rural college-bound students. In 2002, the average annual college tuition was 77.3% of an average family's income in the urban area, and 177.6% of that in the rural area (M. Zhou, 2007). For urban students whose families are less sensitive to price change in HE, expansion means widened access. They are relieved from the "teaching-to-tests" mode of education, and are able to devote more time to extracurricular activities and hobbies. In rural secondary schools, in anticipation of unaffordable college tuitions and decreased return on their educational investments (as a result of the deflation of university degrees) (F. L. Li, X. H. Ding, & Morgan, 2009, p.380), more students drop out of high schools, or decline college education even after receiving admission letters. Yan and Chang (2008) conclude that the expansion policy favors rich students. As a result, there is a substantial increase of high-SES background students and decrease of their low-income counterparts in the student population. HE has turned into "a luxurious good affordable only to rich people" (p. 176).

Quality. Given the short time frame between the policy

proposals in April and policy adoption in September, universities were struck by unpreparedness. In actuality, according to Yan and Chang (2008), there was only a 20-day span between MoE's convening the meeting, drafting the policy and its ensuing implementation, which indicates the policy's detachment from the reality of universities' capability of accommodating the sudden growth of student population. The aggressive expansion occurred on top of a system whose facilities had already stretched thin in meeting students' needs. Between 1999 and 2006, governmental provisions for universities and faculty body had increased by 100% respectively, while the total student body had increased by 5 to 6 times (D. Y. Chen, 2002). C. L. Yang's (2007) research indicates that in this time frame, the average building area each student shared decreased from 45.2 to 32.8 square meters. The per student expenditure decreased from ¥6,775 to ¥5,376, a 21% decrease unadjusted for inflation. In 2006, the average STR reached 17.79:1, whereas the optimal ratio is agreed to be 13:1. In some worst case scenarios, STR might hit 40:1 (Zeng & Niu, 2009). Humanities and social science disciplines enrolled more students, as education in these disciplines is less limited by infrastructure as science and technological disciplines. Thus the former are more upfront to the criticisms of offering poor-quality education.

Graduate unemployment. A foreseeable consequence of expansion policy is the "educated unemployment" of university graduates. It has become an increasingly pressing social problem since 2003, and finally forced the termination of expansion in 2006 (Y. Ma & Qin, 2008; Lai & Tian, 2005, 2009). Lai and Tian (2009) cite research statistics from Indian and Spain, arguing that labor markets are naturally too saturated to absorb excessive graduates as a result of aggressive university expansion, according to these precursor countries' experiences, although these facts are overlooked by top policymakers and economists in their obsession with short-term economic gains. In China, the graduate employment rate was around 90% in 2002, whereas it plummeted to 70% in 2003, as the first batch of expanded students exited universities. In 2007, there were 1.44 million unemployed university graduates, who were competing with the 5.59 million new graduates in 2008. Stern as these statistics are, more stern it would be if we differentiate the unemployment rate by type of institutions and by major. For instance, a survey research conducted at universities in Shanxi province suggests that, in 2008, while employment rate among graduates from national flagship universities maintains a level of around 80%, the rate among graduates from local institutions was much lower. Furthermore, the employment rate among graduates in liberal arts and social sciences such as literature and media studies is below 60%, significantly lower than that among science or technological majors. This suggests that certain segments of student population are more profoundly affected by the expansion policy. The graduate unemployment rate has entered national policy agenda as an urgent and critical issue pertaining to social stability (C. L. Yang, 2007).

Although some optimistic view regards graduate unemployment as "voluntary unemployment" that can be alleviated, if not solved, by multiple adjunct policies (Han, Weng, & B. Zhou, 2007; T. Wang & Zeng, 2009; K. M. Wu & Lai, 2004; K. M. Wu & Sun, 2005; Zeng, 2004), the central government reacted by curtailing undergraduate expansion and installing graduate expansion. Many theorists believe that HE is far from producing sufficient number of university graduates to meet economic needs; the graduate unemployment rate, rather than being attributable to university expansion, is caused by multiple other factors, such as the segmentation of labor market, information asymmetry, students' unrealistic expectations, poor quality in university instructions and career counseling services. One example they cite is that most highly-educated talents concentrate on the coastal or southern regions, leaving the vast Western China and rural areas depleted of high-quality human resources. For instance, in a 2002 survey, 45% of university graduates intended to work and live in coastal areas. When such expectations are unrealized, students will withhold employment temporarily, thus creating a pattern termed "voluntary unemployment" (Lai & Tian, 2009). Although these theorists make multiple suggestions as how to smooth away the aftermath of university expansion, the central government decided to curtail undergraduate expansion in 2006, replacing it with aggressive plans in expansion of graduate-student admissions (Yan & Chang, 2008).

In short, through analyzing the *contexts*, *texts* and *consequences* of the two national HE policies, amalgamation and expansion, one can gain a better understanding of how these policies are neoliberal-ideology driven, while simultaneously top-down, emanating from the national (sometimes international) centers. Both policies center on economic rationality, seeking to maximize usage of economic resources or universities' productive capacity. In both cases, universities' roles and functions limit to reducing costs, producing economically productive talents, alleviating unemployment rate, contributing to national GDP, etc., as if other social good does not matter. Furthermore, both policies are generated among a coterie of elites (top political leaders and economists) and enforced top-down by the MoE, in a "thunderbolt" and non-consensus seeking manner, and have a lasting and profound impact on the HE landscape despite the resistance. In both cases, it is not conclusive if stipulated goals are achieved. This case-study research seeks to amplify a single university's perspective that is suppressed and silenced in the national grand narrative of economy and efficiency. It intends to evaluate the "situated practices" of these two policies at the university of focus, through conducting phenomenological interviews. The findings pertaining to amalgamation and expansion will be presented in Chapter 4.

Chinese National Quality Assurance Policies

In this second part of Chapter 2, I provide background information on national teaching and research quality assurance mechanisms. Unlike amalgamation and expansion, national quality assurance policies are more prevalent in the international arena, and have less direct impacts on people at the institutional level, although they infiltrate and become part of the institutions' normal operations. I follow the trajectory of policy dynamics from the international level, through the national level to their landing at the university of focus, where the ideologies and logics underlying national quality assurance policies are institutionalized and become operationalized in the university's internal mechanisms like the Dudao Team and faculty promotion.

In this part of literature review, I first describe the accountability movements in the international arena, by reference to which the discussions on Chinese national quality control system, its co-option of university internal mechanisms and ensuing resistance (discussed in Chapter 5) can be illuminated. Drawing heavily from the work of David Dill (1997), Martin Trow (1994, 1996a, 1996b) and others, I discuss the heavy usage of quality assurance mechanisms—referred to as the rise of "audit culture" in HE (Shore & Wright, 2000)—and its impact, the "deprofessionalization" of academic professions in Western "core" countries (e.g., the United States, Britain, and other European countries) where most research is produced. Quality assurance mechanisms in other areas (e.g., some other Asian countries) are mentioned but not reviewed in depth due to the scarcity of research.

Second, I explain the teaching and research quality assurance mechanisms at Chinese national level and unravel the embedded goals these mechanisms bear. That is, the "performance indicators" enforced in national teaching and research quality policies embody international integration and nation building agenda. I will further argue that these quality assurance mechanisms either impact on the university people directly, or indirectly by co-opting the university's internal mechanisms, like Dudao Team and faculty promotion. All these constitute a source for the university people's critical reflections and resistance in Chapter 5.

The Rising "Audit Culture" and "Deprofessionalization" of Academics.

The audit explosion in the international arena. This part of literature scans briefly the frenzy towards quality control—the rise of "audit culture" in HE—and the "deprofessionalization" of academic professions in the geographic "core" areas (e. g., the United States, Britain and other European countries) as well as some other parts of the world, despite the scarcity of existing research pertaining to the latter. The patterns of quality control and professional responses in the international arena provide a framework for understanding how stringent national quality control filters down to institutional level, and how the university people react and resist at the university of focus in China (Chapter 5).

In the past 30 years, among many changes that have occurred to HE systems in the United States, Britain and other European countries in the neoliberal contexts, the changing relationship between public institutions and their supporting societies is one of the most prominent: there is a retreat of the trust accorded to public institutions. Universities are constantly held accountable for "value for money" as well as for "quality" (Trow, 1996a). They tend to be measured, assessed and judged by external agencies and stakeholders, for "institutional effectiveness" "research productivity" or "teaching performance", in the name of restoring public "impersonal trust" on HE institutions (Hoecht, 2006; Trow, 1996b), or "improving" quality and "empowering" academic staffs. Such phenomenon is referred to as the rise of "audit culture" or "audit explosion" in the literature (Power, 1997; Shore & Wright, 1999, 2000; Ranson, 2003).

In the United States, accountability and quality assessments are traditionally carried out by a "triad" of federal government, state governments, and six regional accreditation bodies (Rhoades & Sporn, 2002). There was a dramatic enhancement of the federal role in quality control of HE in 1992, as the then new *Higher Education Amendments* demanded that "the States create State Postsecondary Review Entities (SPREs) with responsibility for reviewing the quality of all postsecondary institutions and their eligibility for federal student financial aid" (Dill, 1997, p. 16). Although the SPREs initiative was abolished due to the election of a new Congress in 1994, the pressure for tighter quality audit of public HE lingered in individual States' legislations and practices (Trow, 1996a). For instance, according to Dill, since 1992, 10 States have regularly assessed public HE according to "performance indicators," and tied the results to funding, as he comments that "the quality assurance policies and practices of the States are becoming stronger and more complex" (p. 22).

In Britain, formal accountability is stronger and more direct in that the national government is not only holding HE institutions financially accountable, but also discharging quality assessments at institutional, departmental and program levels for funding purposes, or reviews of teaching quality in institutions using monolithic national standards (Henkel, 2000; Morley, 2002, 2003). Different external quality assessments alternate with each other in successive years, as Shore and Wright (2000) lament that "universities experience [d] a veritable panopticon of inspection, with Academic Audit (AA) one year, a competitive Research Assessment Exercise (RAE) another and Teaching Quality Assessment (RQA) the next" (p. 70). Furthermore, according to Brenna and Shah's (2000a, 2000b) observations of 14 OECD member countries, similar national systems of quality assessments have prevailed in Europe. All the evidence points to the rise of "audit culture" or "audit explosion."

In addition, Kells (1999) provides invaluable perspectives on the quality assurance policies in some other parts of the world, such as Latin America, Europe, Asia and Africa, in which the author has involvement through "site visits, policy analysis, questioning and training for participants in the system (but not the designer and implementer)" (p. 220). He further confirms the prevalence of quality assurance mechanisms in these places on which research is very rare.

> There is a wide range in sponsorship and control of the national evaluation schemes: with about one-third of the twenty countries in this study clearly having government control or a high level of government control of the scheme, with about one third having an independent agency with government funding and about one third with no government sponsorship or control, most usually in the form of an agency supported by the institutions themselves (p. 214).

Kells (1999) further describes in detailed research quality assurance mechanism he has personal experience with, although he does not specify which one it is.

> ...in an effort to increase research output and to raise faculty salaries, [an evaluation is conducted on] research output by professors in recent years. They counted the

publications, drew an arbitrary line of acceptable number and paid salary bonuses to those professors with more than the acceptable number, with no payments with less. They then compounded the madness, all conducted under the guise of improvement, by sorting the institution overall productivity level and publishing a league table about it all, doing damage all the way around. This was matched recently in Asia when a new, reform-minded minister decides to quickly evaluate and grade, publicly, all universities. (p. 220)

The rise of "audit culture" in a global scale can be attributed to multiple factors (Hochet, 2006; Trow, 1994, 1996a). The most immediate factor, according to Brennan and Shah (2000a, 2000b), is the large-scale expansion compounded with diminishing governmental and social support for HE in many systems across the world. Accountability and quality assurance mechanisms are adopted to ensure that academic programs are running properly and to generate data for public uses (Harvey & Newton, 2004). Through such mechanisms, universities acquire legitimacy in the public eye (Trow, 1996b) or are forced to examine introspectively their own problems.

A deeper reason, however, is the rise of managerial and corporate culture in which universities are reshaped in the image of private entities and "adopt the private entities' concept of quality as well" (Houston, 2008, p. 62). Discourses on control and compliance infiltrate in. Universities are not only required to account for proper spending of public resources, the "value for money," but also to adopt private sector conceptualization of quality, which involves improvement of efficiency, and "maintaining and improving their [universities'] viability in the market" (p. 62). For instance, Rhoades and Sporn (2002) maintain that quality of education in the United States is aligned with academic programs' market values, but not with the scholarly or disciplinary judgments. Decisions on funding cut in the areas of education or liberal arts are made on basis of the programs' lack of market viability, but not on their lack of "quality" from scholarly perspectives.

Hochet's (2006) explanation of the "audit explosion" is that, in today's society, public institutions and professional expertise and advice are viewed more with suspicion and distrust. Heavy usage of accountability and quality assurance measures, in most cases by governments, helps to restore an "impersonal trust" on public institutions. Furthermore, by making their subordinate institutions more accountable, governments "can act as guardians of the public interest, distract from any deficiency they may have in terms of their own accountability" (p. 545). In short, it is the desire for control and enforcing compliance rather than for improvement that gives rise to the "audit culture" across the world's HE systems (Harvey & Newton, 2004).

"Deprofessionalization" of academic professionals. As the definition of "quality" is highly subjective, and to a large extent tied to a viewer's purposes and standing point (Brennan & Shah, 2000a; Findlow, 2008; Kells, 1999; Harvey & Newton, 2004; Newton, 2002), the imposition of quality standards—the "performance indicators"—of one party on another is highly political and suggestive of hierarchical power relations (Shore & Wright, 1999, 2000). The fact that most quality assessments are discharged by governments (Houston, 2008) has profoundly transformed the social relations in individuals institutions and in academic disciplines, traditionally considered either as communities of scholars or as loose aggregations of like-minded professionals (Peters, 1992). What the "audit explosion" affects most is the power and status of academic professionals, which Shore and Wright (1999) and Trow (1994) term as the "deprofessionalization" of academic professionals.

Brennan and Shah (2000a) maintain that the application of external quality measures on universities significantly alters existing power structures by strengthening the institutional management. In external quality assessments, the management is provided with "information [of which] to base decisions and an external 'threat' to justify the need to make those decisions" (p. 346). In contrast, senior academics lose most of their powers in institutional decision-making.

According to Shore & Wright (1999), quality assurance mechanisms are creating social distance and hierarchy within disciplines. Academic disciplines are traditionally considered as loose aggregations of like-minded professionals or as "guilds" (Barnett, 2000). Brennan and Shah (2000a) describe that the disciplines are depending on "collective understanding between academics... that a particular piece of work counts as good and something else as less good. Without that collective understanding academic disciplines really do not exist" (p. 346). In the rise of "audit culture," peer review is increasingly used to "police" and monitor colleagues on behalf of external assessors, so as to increase disputes, inconsistencies and social hierarchies among professionals.

Shore and Wright (2000) continue to argue that although external audit works to reshape institutional and disciplinary structures they apply to, they have the greatest impacts on academics' professional, collegial and personal identities. In the "audit explosion", professional autonomy and academic freedom, which traditionally are only subject to peer process and pursuit of knowledge, now are experiencing external scrutiny and control. Academics lose, to a considerable degree, autonomy and discretion in their own work, while are obliged to perform their work in accordance to externally defined "performance" or "productivity" indicators. The audit processes reconstruct individuals as self-actualizing, self-managed agents that set their own standards and goals of performance and productivity. On the surface, academics are "empowered" or orient towards improvement; in actuality, they are rendered unable to articulate goals and standards that fall out of external assessors' or the institution's definitions, so that "changing the terms of reference is not an option" (p. 62).

Critics disagree on the degrees to which the discourses on quality audit are apt to reshape individual conducts and instill patterned professional behaviors. To some, academics are obliged to present themselves in the language and discourses of external assessors' to a degree that conditions of work and thoughts are severely constrained. Shore and Wright (1999, 2000) maintain that academics have turned from "subjects in communications" into "objects of information" in academic-audit process. Trow (1994) comments that academic staffs are transformed into "mere organizational personnel", who are "interested in promotion and better pay as rewards for better performance as determined by external assessors against yardsticks supplied by government agencies" (p. 30).

To some others, academics coping with external academic audit merely engage in "outward conformity," as Trowler (2001) describes that the quality discourses do not change "for a minute what is in [academic's] hearts and minds" (p. 183). For instance, the faculty members in Hochet's (2006) study merely view answering to external assessors as a way to "play the game" rather than "betray themselves or sell their personality" (p. 56; see also Henkel, 2000; Morley, 2002, 2003). Nevertheless, traditional sense of professional autonomy and academic freedom is significantly altered in the "audit explosion."

Chinese national teaching and research quality assurance mechanisms.

Vidovich et al. (2007) comment that, in the past 20 years, Chinese governmental regulation and control of HE escalate in that "Chinese universities are subjected to unprecedented external scrutiny" (p. 93). Despite the rhetoric of "decentralization", Chinese government shifts from direct management to "steering at distance" through quality assurance mechanisms on teaching and research. The 1999 Higher Education Act (MoE, 1999) has mandateed that HE institutions answer to educational governing bodies, while the government may rightfully choose to withhold information, such as the methodologies and results of quality assessments, from the public. The fact that accountability is asymmetrical and not reciprocated by the government greatly enhances governmental control over HE (J. Li & Yan, 2008).

In this part of literature, I briefly introduce different quality assurance mechanisms and continue to argue that these mechanisms seek to reshape and orient institutions towards governmental agenda such as international integration and nation building. This literature helps the readers understand my further analysis of how these mechanisms impact on the university of focus directly and indirectly, which constitutes a condition of the university people's coping and resistance.

National teaching quality assurance mechanisms. The 2003 report by Organization for Economic Co-operation and Development (OECD) relatively summarizes the quality assurance mechanisms in China in a thorough way. Teaching quality assurances mechanisms are summarized as follows, among which the most notable is the once-five-year "national undergraduate teaching evaluation," first discharged by MoE in 2003.

(1) Academic Degree Committee of the State

Council is responsible for defining the differentiated standards for the degrees of Bachelor, Master and Doctor.

(2) The Higher Education Department of the MoE has established a Disciplinary Guidance Committee whose task is to define the academic standards of Bachelor Degrees in all disciplines (curricula and content) for recognition of academic titles and certificates. A pool of 700 experts is involved in defining the specific requirements for all disciplines of higher studies.

(3) A committee for Accreditation, supported by the Educational Development and Planning Division, defines the qualification procedures for assessing the educational capacities of individual HE institutions in order to grant permission for establishing Higher Educational Institutions.

(4) The Academic Degree Committee of the State Council is responsible for examining the qualification of the HE institutions and research institutes to offer academic degrees. (p. 24)

In 2003, a new procedure, the once-5-year national teaching evaluation, was put in place. The teaching evaluation is criterion-referenced in that it compares observed teaching performance against pre-set "performance indictors" determined by MoE, which include 7 indices (further divided into 19 sub-indices), covering institutions' mission statements, faculty force, facilities, management, etc (MoE, 2004b, 2004c). Each institution in the nation is assessed following three steps: an institution first conducts self-assessment in reference to "performance indictors." Then, a group of experts visit and inspect the institution and finally, the institution takes a one-year period to work on self-improvement in accordance to external assessors' advise. By the first half of 2008, 592 HE institutions have been evaluated, with each demanded to submit to MoE a report on improvement after one year of the assessment (Yu & A. B. Xie, 2008; F. Wang & Hu, 2009). The underlining assumption of national undergraduate teaching evaluation is that, according to J. L. Zhang (2009), the outcomes of teaching can be guaranteed, with each step in teaching process standardized. The national undergraduate teaching evaluation occurs in a context of drastic university expansion and reduction in governmental support to HE. It is argued in official terms that the teaching evaluation functions to restore public trust in university education and force the universities to look introspectively at their own problems, despite academics' virulent criticisms and resistance against it (J. Li & Yan, 2008; Shen, 2006).

National research quality assurance mechanisms. Research quality is maintained through mechanisms like graduate program accreditation and the regular review and assignment of "first-grade" disciplines and laboratories (OECD, 2003; Shen, 2006). In the graduate program accreditation, according to OECD, "approval of doctoral and professional programs [is] given by MoE. The provincial Education Commissions have the authority to decide on the establishment of Master-level and undergraduate programs" (p. 24). The MoE reviews of "first-grade" disciplines assess the research performance at department level regularly, with generous funding dispatched towards those departments and disciplines assigned with "first-grade" status (M. Q. Lin, X. J. Zhou & Zhen, 2005). Across all national research assessments, the heavy usage of number of international journal publications, national research grants and contest rewards as "performance indictors" is suggestive of the international integration and national building goals embedded in these assessments.

International integration has been the dominant theme in Chinese HE reform discourse since Jiang Zeming's speech in 1998 (Mohrman, 2005, 2008; R. Yang, 2004). Vidovich et al.

(2007) comment that the ambition to create "world-class" universities in China "set [s] the framework for understanding changes to accountability policy and practices" (p. 94). As the prestige and status of a university system largely depends on the visibility of its researchers, publications in international journals, such as Science Citation Index (SCI) and Social Science Citation Index (SSCI) journals, have high viability across all research assessments, be it accreditation of programs, or evaluation of disciplines. To enhance the values and "productivity" of their programs or disciplines in the eyes of evaluators, it is a common practice among institutions to pay high prizes to encourage scholars to publish in international journals with high "impact factors," such as *Nature* and *Science* (Tao, 2002). Given the language impediment, and the collective "Aphasia" of humanities and social science scholars in the international arena, higher values were signed to publications in SSCI than in Chinese Social Science Index (CSSCI) journals (a Chinese equivalent of SSCI). For instance, at Beijing and Qinghua Universities, professors receive high rewards for SSCI publications (N. Wang, 2006).

Altbach (2001, 2004) criticizes the international knowledge system as highly centralized and exclusive, with the top internationally-circulating journals concentrating in a few developed countries and only in favor of those who are familiar with the scholarly norms and the language in the "core" geographic area. In short, in an effort to "break into 'major leagues' of science in the world" (Altbach, 2001, p. 199), Chinese government reinforces a biased research evaluative system, where the quality of research is judged by itself, as well as by the geographical locales where journals are edited, and by the language the research uses (R. Yang, 2004). As a result, research topics irrelevant or recognized as unimportant to the international research communities are marginalized and silenced. Mohrman (2005) comments that in emulating the world's centers of excellence or "world-class universities", China unnecessarily abandons its traditional strength in social sciences research, and Yang laments that indigenous research is at stake and sacrificed in China's strives for international integration.

In addition to international integration, the national research evaluation systems have persistently oriented towards enhancing universities' roles in economic development and political stability. Competitive governmental grants, for instance, have born the similar missions as federal grants in the United States. According to Rhoades and Sporn (2002), in the United States, federal influence or control in HE resides in providing funding for research so as to shape academic programs and fields of research towards a direction that is conducive to U.S. economy and global competitiveness. The quality of federally-funded research has been guaranteed by a peer review process, so that federal funding has higher prestige and status among a hierarchy of different types of grants (Dill, 1997; Slaughter & Rhoades, 2004). In a similar fashion in China, the prestige of governmental funding (termed "vertical grants") is ordered in accordance to the administrative hierarchy of funding sources, for instance, the grant from MoE is naturally of higher rank than those from provincial educational bureaus. At the bottom of the hierarchy is funding from non-governmental sources, like industries (termed "horizontal" grants).

Apart from journal publications and governmental grants, the number of official research contest awards is another important "performance indictor" in national quality assessments of research. Each year, the national, provincial and local governments administer all kinds of contests of research in natural sciences, technologies, social sciences and humanities. For instance, for social sciences and humanities, MoE organizes a National Outstanding Award For Humanities and Social Sciences, and

Jiangsu province offers an Outstanding Award for Fruits in Philosophy and Social Sciences. As G. Y. Zhang and Y. Luo (2007) and H. Y. Liu (2005), comparing the different practices in foreign countries and China, conclude that in China, awards from governmental sources are much more honorable and prestigious than those from other sources, such as scholarly communities and industries. For instance, at the international arena, the highest and ultimate recognition of scholarly and research work, the Nobel Prizes, are from the researchers' own communities. In China, a certain research community has to align itself with a governmental bureau, in order to validate itself in other people's eyes.

Although the legitimacy and authority of both competitive governmental grants and research contests are considered to be maintained through peer reviews, the peer status of government-invited scholars and administrators is highly questionable (H. B. Gu & B. Y. Wang, 2004). These peers are evaluating research proposals or scholarly work, using not the "collective understanding" of the disciplines, but the rules and guidelines issued by the governmental bureaus, as Shen (2006) states that "they [peers] are representatives of the government but not their HE institutions or scholarly communities. They are answering to the former but not the latter" (p.4). They tended to be referred to as "experts" rather than "peers" in both the official and unofficial lexicon. Sleeboom (2004) criticizes the tendency of reinforcing "nation-centered" research policies in China. That is, the quality of natural sciences research is defined by its relevance to national economy and social sciences research to political stability. The governmental grants and contests are charged with reinforcing these agenda.

In short, in this part of literature review, I briefly summarized national quality assurance mechanisms in China, and how the "performance indictors" enforced embody hidden agenda such as international integration and nation building. In Chapter 5, I will embark on explaining that the national teaching and research quality mechanisms have both direct and indirect impacts on the university of focus. Apart from the direct impact, the national quality assurance mechanisms tend to co-opt normal university functions and turn them into stretched mechanisms of surveillance and control. The university's Dudao Team and faculty promotion policies are two examples. One part of Chapter 5 will be devoted to demonstrating that the same "performance indicators" in national research quality assurance mechanisms are institutionalized in the way the university of focus chooses to measure faculty performance and sets promotion criteria, which constitutes a source for faculty critical reflections and resistance.

Summary

In Chapter 2, the literature review chapter, I provided background information on the HE reform policies in this case-study research. I first illustrated the *contexts*, *texts* and *consequences* of amalgamation and expansion policies, in relation to which university people's lived experiences with amalgamation and expansion in Chapter 4 should be read. I then examined various national quality assurance mechanisms by following the trajectory of policy dynamics from the international to national level. In Chapter 5, I will further demonstrate how the "audit culture" infiltrates at the institutional level, and constitutes a context for university people's resistance and coping.

Chapter 3
Methods

In Chapter 3, I will describe in detail the concrete process through which the research was conducted: what was the setting like? What was the researcher' role in the research? How were participants identified and selected? How were data collected and analyzed? In the description, I wave in and out literature that supported the particular actions I took in the research. As each methodological practice has its philosophical underpinnings and corresponds to a particular set of ontological and epistemological orientations, I intend to make my philosophic assumptions explicit, especially that this case-study uses phenomenological interviews (Seidman, 2006) as a methodological approach. Phenomenological research is unique, and by drawing heavily on Seidman, Karlsson (1993), Guba and Lincoln (1994), and Yanow (2006) that have strong phenomenological roots, I try to justify my methodology in the eyes of those who insist on "triangulation" of data sources.

Setting

The university of focus in this case-study research, whose main campus situates at the center of a large city in China, is one of the oldest and most prestigious "key" universities in China. It was first established in the early 19th century as a normal university, when the reform-minded bureaucrats in late Qing dynasty (1636—1911) were mass importing Western-style higher learning institutions, on top of the indigenous learning mechanism, as a way to revitalize Chinese culture (Bastid, 1987; Curran, 2005; Hayhoe, 1996; Pepper, 1996; Weston, 2004). Universities that trace their histories back to the late Qing period usually have secured fame and status in China. The university of focus has weathered all turbulences and changes ever since. In the Nationalist era (1927—1949) in China, the university was known as one of the nationally renowned universities. After the establishment of the People's Republic of China in 1949, during the period that Hartnett (1996) terms as Chinese "mindless copying" of Soviet Union learning system, the university was reestablished as an institution of technology, with its natural sciences, social sciences and liberal arts units severed from it and integrated into other institutions. What were left were the "core" applied-science departments like architecture, civil engineering, electronics and information technology, which were still considered as the representative units of the university of focus today.

The university of focus in this case study has a "key" status, a top-30 university in both official and unofficial terms. In China, there are two coexisting yet asymmetrical (the official and unofficial) ways of designating a university "key" status. First, a university's status is defined by its "belonging." The large-scale 1952—1957 HE restructuring in history co-opted an overwhelming majority of Chinese universities into the public system, leaving very few outliers like the "people-run" colleges. The public universities are respectively governed and managed by three types of governmental bodies: The MoE, central and local specialized ministries (e.g. Ministry of Finance, Ministry of Agriculture, Ministry of Medicine) and local (provincial or municipal) governments. Those under the direct jurisdiction of the MoE, usually locating in large cities, are the "key" universities with prestige and high status. In 1999, there were 45 such key universities out of a total of 1,071 regular HE institutions (X. F. Wang, 2003) whereas by 2006, the rate shifted towards 73 out of 1,867 (MoE, 2009a). The increase in the raw number of key universities is due to the fact that the specialized ministries are conferring universities under their jurisdiction to either MoE or local governments, mandated by the 1993 *Outlines* (MoE, 1993). In addition to the official system of university ranking, there are around five non-governmental institutions in China that publish "league tables" of university rankings each year. Such rankings, claiming to have adopted international criteria and methodologies, are influencing, albeit to a limited degree, governmental decisions on funding or ordinary people's conception of quality and excellence (N. C. Liu & L. Liu, 2005). Although the official and unofficial systems of status designation are claimed to be independent of each other, the ranking lists they produce each year overlap to a great extent (Vidovich et al., 2007).

As I have argued in the introductory chapter that this research is an instrumental case study (Stake, 1995), in which the study of the case is an instrument for understanding an issue, the implementation or "situated practices" of national HE reform policies and university innovative practices. The case chosen as a case of focus needs to be "typical" and "representative" through which the researcher is able to find out as much as possible about the "issue" (Merriam, 1998). I argue that the university of focus serves as an ideal site in that, besides being a key university and the recipient of 211 and 985 funding, the university has a history of faithfully implementing the national HE reform policies since the Chinese economic liberation in 1978, such as building comprehensive universities, building second-grade/autonomous colleges, building new campuses, and merger.

Since the late 1980s, the university has been restructuring its natural sciences, social sciences, and liberal arts departments, adding to its technological core departments such as law, literature, philosophy and economics. This move was in conjunction with the national policy climate of building comprehensive universities, in a nation-wide effort to reverse the overspecialization handed down from the Soviet models. In 2000 the university of focus amalgamated with three other institutions, acquiring three additional campuses, including a medical school. In 2003, it established an adjunct "second-grade" college, a private sector in addition to its public core (renamed "autonomous" college in 2004). In the summer of 2006, the university completed the construction of a new campus in the suburb of the city, which was 3 times in size in comparison to its old campus. The new campus has hosted all undergraduate and graduate programs, leaving the old campus to function merely as administrative and research units.

The university is developing, since the 1980s, towards a comprehensive, gigantic, "aircraft-carrier" type of institution, in convergence to the national goal of building world-class universities. In actuality, the university was awarded both 211 and 985 grants. The 211 Project is a governmental effort to develop around 100 top universities for the 21st century; in realization that China will probably fail to develop 100 internationally-recognized institutions, at least in the short run, the Chinese government adopted the 985 Project instead as a conscious strategy to concentrate resources on a handful of institutions with the greatest potentials for success in the international academic marketplace (MoE, 2004a, 2010). It might be safe to stipulate that the university of focus has a tight relationship with the government, faithfully implementing governmental reform initiatives. It serves as an ideal site for scrutinizing how an institution responds to and how people at the university experience changes under the national HE reform policies.

By the time I was visiting the university of focus during

November 2008 and January 2009, the university has altogether 6 campuses: one old, 3 acquired through merger, one newly built, and one private-sector campus which surprisingly stresses its "autonomous" status to the university. As my initial interviews conducted on the autonomous campus suggested that it was somehow independent from the university, using the university's brand name, but not administratively affiliated, I did not include the autonomous section in my further study. This case-study research was conducted on the 5 campuses. The "autonomous" college unaccounted, the university covers a total area of 155 hectares, and boasts over 40 schools or departments with 60 undergraduate disciplines in all. It also has 15 post-doctoral stations, and offers 105 Ph. D. programs and 200 Master's programs. The total number of faculty and staff is 6,000, including 1,500 full or associate professors, 300 doctoral supervisors, 7 academicians of the Chinese Academy of Sciences and Chinese Academy of Engineering. The number of full-time students reaches 26,000, with around 10,000 of them enrolled in graduate-level programs. Part-time students add up to 3,000.

Researcher Positionality

The impact of the researcher as a "key tool for fieldwork" has long been recognized in social-science research (Reinharz, 1997; Hertz, 1997). The researcher's subjectivity is imposed on every stage of the research, in the "doing" as well as "writing" —from the questions asked, the participants chosen, to the analysis, representation and writing up of the texts. Therefore, instead of trying to check or bracket out researcher effects, it is important to include the researcher's self reflections in relation to the respondents and to the contexts under study—self-analysis, autobiographic sketches, personal standing—into qualitative studies. With these elements included in the research, the readers are able to situate the researcher in the study and have insights into how the knowledge about the respondents comes into existence (Alsup, 2004; Hertz, 1997; Sanger, 2003).

While self-reflexivity is important for all types of qualitative research, it is especially indispensible for phenomenological interviews, which, at the roots, are the understanding of "the lived experience of other people and the meaning they make of that experience" (Seidman, 2006, p.9), or "enter[ing] the lifeworld of the interviewees" (Lofmark, Morberg, Ohlund & Ilicki, 2009, p. 114). The researcher may take actions to minimize his or her effects on the participants' reflection on or reconstruction of experiences in the research process. Given the emphasis on a priori knowledge in phenomenology, the researcher is seen to bring personal history into the interviews, and meaning is a function of the social interaction between the researcher and the researched. Seidman paraphrases Schutz (1967) that a researcher can never understand a participant perfectly, as, "to do so would mean that we had entered into the other's stream of consciousness and experienced what he or she had. If we could do that, we would be that other person" (p.9). Thus Guba and Lincoln (1994) view the research process as interaction and negotiation between the researcher and the researched, and the end product as the consensus reached between the two sides—which leads to a more sophisticated understanding of the world. The researcher inevitably brings his or her own history to the interviews; he or she makes sense of what other people tell by drawing on the richness of his or her own personal experiences. The interviews might echo or revoke parts of the researcher's life. Given this understanding, it is not only desirable but compulsory to provide reflections on the researcher's social and cultural positions in relation to the respondents and the contexts under study, as the researcher's personal history and interactions with the respondents are inevitably part of the data generated. Thus an autobiographical section explaining the researcher's connection to his or her proposed research is recommended by Seidman (2006), Maxwell (2005) and Yanow (2006).

I consider myself strategically positioned in the insider-outsider continuum vis-à-vis the respondents and the contexts under study. Studying a university is inevitable when it comes to choosing the subject matter, as universities have been my primary life context. As my father has worked as a humanities faculty for over 30 years, respectively at two large universities in a large Chinese city, our family has lived in apartments on the campuses where he has been working. I was born and grew up on campus, with all my playmates, and the elders I was socializing with in one way or another connected to universities. I obtained my undergraduate and graduate degrees during a 7-year period from a prestigious Chinese university in the same city, and worked very briefly, for half a year, as a faculty member in the English department of a technological institution in the same city. In 2002, I came to the United States and started a prolonged process of studying and socializing at Arizona State University. After obtaining my doctoral degree, I look forward to locating a position as a faculty member either in the United States or China, which probably will be my life-long career. So universities have been my primary (and only) life context and an inescapable choice when it comes to making a decision on the research topic.

I regard myself as an "insider" to the university of focus, despite that my intensive fieldwork lasted only 3 months. I had lived on the campus of the university of focus for several years before 2002, with particular knowledge about humanities faculty members and students. I had been socializing with some of them for a long time, knowing, how, "in concrete and ordinary ways, [this group of] intellectuals have lived" (Weston, 2004, p. 10). In other words, my level of familiarity with most of the interview participants did not rest on their ideas and concepts, but on how they dress, network, carry our ceremonies and spend leisure. Before 2002, I had been socializing with the university people, with whom I have

> ...a long history of sharing common experiences. These shared experiences have over time led to the creation of the shared view of the world... This shared view enables people in the organization to make sense of commonplace as well as usual events, ascribe meaning to symbols and rituals, and share in a common understanding of how to deal with the unfolding action in appropriate ways. (Owens, 1998, p. 267)

The themes that emerged through the analysis, such as university-government dyad, faculty members' coping with and resistance to top-down, outside-in reforms, and frontline academic staffs' engagement with innovative practices, are reverberating with what have been lingering on my mind for years. Locke, Silverman, Spirduso (2004) state that all qualitative research has its autobiographical roots. It was my personal history and experience with the university of focus that motivated my choice of the topic, and sustained me through the "labor-intensive" process of data collection, analysis and research writing.

Simultaneously, I am an "outsider" to the university of focus. Seidman (2006) states that the researcher needs to have sufficient social distance from the researched so as to "be open to the process of listening and careful exploration" (p. 32), and approach his or her research with "a certain sense of naiveté, innocence and absence of prejudgments" (p. 33). Miles and Huberman (1994) maintain that, in social-science research, it is important that the researcher be void of "Bias B", that is, getting co-opted in the setting and risking misinterpreting the data to fit into his or her own perceptions, expectations and background. Argyris (1993) especially emphasizes that an organizational researcher should not take for granted what "the actors take for granted" (p. 38); otherwise, the researcher might be unintentionally colluding with the status quo. As a doctoral student who has studied at a U. S. university for years, I somehow achieved the "outsider" status to the university of focus through staying detached from it for years. The experiences at the U. S. university are complex, full of contradictions and ambiguities. On the one hand, it is intellectually inspiring; through years of socialization, I am able to anchor to the broad community of "policy researchers." I am familiar with the standards of judgment, canons of evidence, or normative measures prescribed to this particular community. On the other hand, the experiences at the U. S. university are threatening, involving not only constant struggle for economic survival, but also having to prove to university administrators my "innocence." I have to fill out forms each year to maintain a "legal" status, which constantly reminds me that I am an alien, unwelcome, and temporary to the environment. Both my academic expertise in policy research and my unpleasant encounters with the US political structure, all these unfamiliar experiences accord me an "outsider" status in relation to the university of focus, and enable me to step back while listening to the stories of participants in the case study.

In short, this research is about the university of focus: responses to external reform efforts, and its inside-out innovative practices. The process of conducting and writing up the research is simultaneously a complex playing out of my previous experiences with Chinese universities and current experiences with U. S. universities. Although "I" as an author does not assume an explicit narrative voice in the written text, it is simultaneously everywhere in the research.

Participants

Purposeful sampling is more favored than random sampling in qualitative research (Seidman, 2006). The interview participants in this case-study research were drawn through a combination of "maximum variation" sampling (Patton, 2002) and snow-ball sampling methods. "Maximum variation" is a method in which the researcher attempts to increase the diversity or variations of participants or cases to a maximum extent within a given range. The examples Patten (2002) gives are to cover as wide geographical areas as possible (e.g., urban areas and rural areas) in evaluating academic programs across the nation, or cover as many staff roles as possible so as to understand "variations in experiences" in evaluating a single program. An analogous situation in this case study is that within the confines of the university of focus, I planned to represent administrators, faculty members and students from as many academic and administrative units as possible. Snow-ball sampling refers to a method in which one participant leads to another.

Prior to my visit to the university, I made a matrix, the rows of which consisted of all the departments, offices, and units that I took off the university's home page (e.g., Department of Mathematics, the president's office) and the columns of which consisted of different roles like junior/senior faculty, administrator, staff, undergraduate/graduate student. The square at the conjunction of a row and column indicated a person I wanted to interview. For instance, the intersection of a row consisted of "Department of Mathematics," and a column consisted of "senior faculty" indicated that I wanted to interview a senior faculty in the Department of Mathematics. I tried to spread out the interview participants as much as possible. That is, I tried to fill each square with at least one or two persons, unless the criteria listed in the square could not be met (for instance, there was no student in the president's office). To some extent, the squares in the matrix I made presented the maximum extent of roles and units at the university of focus, as Seidman (2006) suggests "sampl[ing] the widest variation of sites and people within the limits of the study" (p. 53).

As my father has worked as a faculty member for the university of focus for 11 years, I started with the colleagues in his department. At the end of each interview, I routinely asked each participant questions like, "Do you know an administrator in the graduate school?" "Could you introduce a student in the department of technology?" This was typically snow-ball sampling method, and my purpose for asking those questions was to fill up the squares in the matrix I mentioned above. Most of the time, my interviewees offered to name a few persons. Through this combination of "maximum variation" and "snow-ball" sampling methods, I was able to draw 41 participants, covering students, faculty members and administrators in around 25 colleges, departments, offices, and units (cannot accurately calculate because some of them overlap), and each was assigned a pseudonym. There are 13 (31.7%) females and 28 (68.3%) males. Their ages range from 21 to 72, with an average of 35 (see Table 1 for detailed demographic features of the interview participants). The limitation of my methods was that I was not able to reach the top-tier of administration (e.g., president and vice presidents); the highest administrative rank represented in my interviewees was dean. Furthermore, 20 (48.8%) participants were from social sciences/liberal arts departments, as compared to 12 (29.3%) who were from natural sciences/ technological departments, indicating a heavy tilter of my social network. The other 9 (22.0%) were from administrative units.

▶ Chapter 3   Methods

Table 1   Demographic Features of Interview Participants

	Names	Departments/Offices/Units	Roles	Sex	Age
1	Zhao	Department of Politics and Administration	Undergraduate/Senior	M	23
2	Qian	Department of Radio Engineering	Undergraduate/Junior	M	22
3	Sun	Law School	Undergraduate/Senior	F	23
4	Li	Department of Politics and Administration	Undergraduate/Sophomore	F	21
5	Zhou	Department of Politics and Administration	Doctoral Student	M	35
6	Wu	Department of Physics/Radio Engineering	Undergraduate/Sophomore	M	21
7	Zheng	Philosophy and Science Department	Doctoral Student	M	36
8	Wang	School of Economics and Management	Master's Student	M	24
9	Feng	Department of Mechanical Engineer	Master's Student	M	24
10	Chen	Department of Computer Science	Master's Student	M	24
11	Zha	Department of Architecture	Undergraduate/Senior	F	23
12	Bei	College of Arts	Undergraduate	F	23
13	Jiang	Department of Politics and Administration	Associate Professor	M	41
14	Sheng	Department of Chemistry	Doctoral Student	M	27
15	Han	Department of Politics and Administration	Lecturer	F	35
16	Yang	School of Economics and Management	Associate Professor	F	36
17	Zhu	Law School	Lecturer	F	32
18	Qing	Department of Mathematics	Professor/Doctoral Advisor	M	41
19	You	Office of Student Affairs	Director	M	38
20	Xu	Department of Radio Engineering	Associate Professor	M	37

续表

	Names	Departments/Offices/Units	Roles	Sex	Age
21	He	Law School	Professor/Dean/Doctoral Supervisor	M	43
22	Lu	Law School	Associate Professor/Associate Dean	F	41
23	Shi	Department of Mathematics	Associate Professor	M	45
24	Zhang	President's Office	Staff	M	39
25	Kong	Office of Teaching and Research	Director of Subunit of Teaching Evaluation	M	35
26	Cao	Office of Teaching and Research	Vice-Director	M	48
27	Yan	Autonomous/Office of Student Affairs	Director	M	52
28	Hua	Medical College	Undergraduate Student/Senior	M	23
29	Jin	Medical College	Undergraduate Student/Senior	M	24
30	Wei	Department of Politics and Administration	Professor/Vice Secretary General	F	42
31	Tao	School of Humanities	Associate Professor/Associate Dean	F	41
32	Chu	Office of Institutional Research/School of Economics and Management	Director/Vice Secretary General	M	53
33	Qi	Department of Bioscience and Medical Engineering	Secretary General	M	33
34	Xie	Department of Mechanical Engineering	Retired Professor/Director of *Dudao* Team	M	72
35	Zuo	Department of English	Lecturer	F	39
36	Yu	Graduate College	Staff in Office of Graduate student Affairs	F	36
37	Bai	Graduate College	Staff in Office of Disciplinary Development	M	34

续表

	Names	Departments/Offices/Units	Roles	Sex	Age
38	Shui	Graduate College	Staff of Office of Admission	F	29
39	Dou	Office of Public Relations	Vice Director	F	33
40	Yun	Department of Materials	Doctoral Student	M	32
41	Su	Department of Politics and Administration	Professor/Doctoral Advisor	M	63

The interview participants consisted of "ordinary" university people, including administrators, faculty members and students. They are either what the literature terms as "street-level" bureaucrats (deLeon & deLeon, 2002a; Maynard-Moody & Leland, 1999) or ordinary members of the organization. All are at the "receive end" of national HE reform policies.

In most research on university organizations and policy implementation, "key players" are preferred; this research, on the contrary, focuses on "ordinary" people given the underpinning theoretic framework of the research. Mills (2007), for instance, suggests that "the best way to determine and probe the motivation and meanings of policy deliberation is…to talk with the important actors in the process" (p. x). Similarly, Y. M. Wan and Peterson (2007), in their case study of university merger in China, suggest using "purposeful sampling" to draw "information-rich" participants who "were chosen based upon their official standing in their institutions and upon their degree of involvement in and knowledge of the merger process" (p. 686). As a consequence, their study is mainly composed of top-level administrators and academic deans from both institutions they studied. In this case-study research, access to such powerful politicians and senior bureaucrats are particularly difficult for a student conducting research. Furthermore, as I have made clear in Chapter 2, the Literature Review section, this research is about the "situated practices" of national HE reform policies and the inside-out, bottom-up innovative ideas and practices at the university of focus. It is the views from the below—"street-level" administrators, frontline faculty members and students—that count. Thus, I identified and selected administrators, faculty members and students, through a combination of "maximum variation" and "snow-ball" sampling methods, as interview participants in this study.

Data Collection and Analysis

Data collection

Data in this case-study research were collected during an intensive 3-month period between November 2008 and January 2009, through semi-structured interviews. Seidman (2006) maintains that "the adequacy of a research method depends on the purpose of the research and the questions being asked" (p. 11). I first describe what concrete steps I took in the setting to achieve "detached involvement" and justify why I was relying on interview data while explaining how interviews were conducted.

I basically follow Clark's (1998) methodology when he researched the transformation of five European universities. He wrote that

> During each visit, I engaged in about a dozen taped interviews with faculty, administrators, and students, each lasting one to two hours. I also foraged for documents to review and carry away; sat in a few meetings, where possible, and looked around at what was going on in the offices, classrooms, laboratories, corridors, and pathways of the campus. (p. xv)

Although observations and document collections were an

integral part of my data collection, these processes serve to familiarize myself with the organizational process so that meaningful interactions and discourses would not escape my eyes (Gabriel, 1995). That is, I wanted to achieve a state of "detached involvement" (Czarniawska, 1998) with the organization. The data included in the analysis were the interviews with the 41 participants.

As my father works for the university of focus, I had lived in an apartment on the old (main) campus for several years before 2002. During the 90-day intensive fieldwork for this research, I made repeated and regular visits from the main to other five campuses: the other three campuses in close vicinity of the main; and the private-sector campus and the new campus that respectively took around 50-minute bus ride. I excluded the private-sector campus early on. I made on average 10 trips to each of the other campuses, with the new campus caught most of my attention, as the participants repeatedly requested to be interviewed there. My activities to immerse myself in the university's organizational process include: sitting in a few meetings (e.g., the regular bi-weekly faculty meeting in the Department of Politics and Administration, university-wide meetings mobilizing the faculty and students for the MoE's "undergraduate teaching evaluation," university and departmental meetings recognizing outstanding students); collecting policy documents (e.g., from the university's webpage; asking a participant for the sources whenever he or she mentioned a policy change; collecting year books; and collecting books edited by university administrators); taking snap shots of banners, posters, buildings, bulletin boards, etc. Besides, the daily 50-minute bus trip served as an ideal site for overhearing and participating in the discussions of events, anecdotes, gossips, complaints and aspirations concerning the university. As stories permeate every nook and cranny of the organization that "we live in a sea of stories and like the fish who (according to the proverb) will be the last to discover water, we have our own difficulties grasping what it is like to swim in stories" (Rodriguez, 2002), such informal, random engagement with the organization activities was already providing me with overwhelming sources conducive to the research.

Beyond activities that helped me achieve "detached involvement" at the university of focus, I relied primarily on the data obtained from semi-structured interviews with 41 participants for analysis. Seidman (2006) stresses that the way data are collected should be congruent with the purposes of the research and the questions asked. This case study has an "existential" phenomenological framing (Yanow, 2006) in that I intend to search for the lived experiences of university people in relation to national HE reform policies and inside-out, bottom-up change efforts. The process requires the participants to reflect on their streams of experiences, select events and frame them into languages that are meaningful to both the respondents and the listeners (Weick, 1995). Semi-structured interviews that are carried out in an informal conversational manner are an ideal tool for eliciting this type of knowledge.

Furthermore, Seidman (2006) maintains that phenomenological interviews have particular ontological and epistemological underpinnings and do not usually combine with other data collection methods which do not share the same assumptions. In phenomenological framing, the "objective" world becomes intelligent when each "subjective" person experiences it in a unique way. So, according to phenomenology, there is no "objective" world universal to everyone, but only the combination of the "subjective" and "objective," that is, the "objective" world as grasped by consciousness or as experienced by an individual. Karlsson (1993) states that

The object and subject are not two independent and

separate entities. Instead, the subject and object are linked to one another through the notion of "intentionality." In other words, "facts" always presuppose a constituting and meaning-imbuing subject, which excludes the possibility of so-called "pure" facts. (p. 16)

A purpose of "existential" phenomenology is to understand the experienced world, as Deetz (1992) maintains that "there is no route to the world or other persons except through the experience of them" (p. 113). In phenomenological conceptualization, interviews are an ideal method to understand experiences. According to Weick (1995), experience is meaningless, a pure duree of time, until the subject retrospectively "select[s] constitutive details of experience, reflect[s] on them, giv[s] them order and thereby making sense of them" (Seidman, p. 7). The phenomenological interview is not only a channel through which a participant starts to "make sense" of experiences, but also for those experiences to enter into the public realm, and become knowable and discussable by other persons. In short, the interview strategy, especially in a conversational, casual mode, is favored by qualitative studies with phenomenological underpinnings, given this strategy's recognition of multiple subjectivities and insistence on understanding subjectivities from "insider perspective" (Karlsson, 1993, p. 17). In Yanow's (2006) words, through interviews, the researchers are able to "understand from the perspective of the actor in the situation" (p. 13).

Furthermore, phenomenological researchers are not in favor of methodologies that have different assumptions about understanding human experiences. In naturalist observation, for instance, an outside observer may see the physical manifestations of human actions, but cannot understand the meanings and assumptions underlying those actions which can only be tapped through the actors' own accounts and recollection (J. N. Zhang, 2009, 2010).

Trying to understand human actions from "outside the experience itself" is at odds with phenomenological assumptions, as "phenomenological approach does not allow the postulation of such an external frame of reference in its analysis of the experience" (Karlsson, p. 17). Thus, Seidman (2006) maintains that "interviewing provides a necessary, if not always completely sufficient, avenue of inquiry" (p. 11). He further argues that interviews

> When done with skill, can avoid tensions that sometimes arise when a researcher uses multiple methods. That is especially the case when those methods may be based on different assumptions of what it means to understand the experience of others. (p. 6)

On the basis of all these arguments, "triangulation" of methods might not be necessary in phenomenological research.

In short, in this case-study research, I relied primarily on the data yielded through interviews. The advantage of using phenomenological interviews for policy and organizational studies, according to Newton (2002), is that such methodologies "highlight the importance of the views and perspectives of 'front-line' academic staffs engaged in the implementation of policy. They were revealed as 'makers' and 'shapers' in the policy implementation, not mere passive recipients" (p. 48). Yanow (2006) refers to phenomenological interviews as "radically democratic" in that the interview processes accord the status of expertise to the interviewees, as they know "their experiences" and "their lifeworld." The researcher, concerned with "understanding the lifeworld of the actor[s] in the situation(s) being studied" (p. 23), resigns from the traditional role as an expert in the subject matter and assumes a "sustained empathic" attitude in listening to the participants. Phenomenological interviews are a philosophically sound and congruent method to the purposes and research questions of this case-study research.

The interviews with 41 participants took place either on the old or new campus, where I had a borrowed office respectively. Seidman (2006) recommends the "three-interview series" for in-depth phenomenological interviews, in which each of the three interviews lasts around 90 minutes and is 3 days to a week apart. The first interview, according to Seidman, taps the respondents' life contexts, for instance, asking them to reconstruct their early experiences in families, in school, with friends and in neighborhoods. The second interview of the series centers around the concrete details of the participants' present lived experiences in the topic area, and the third interview concentrates on the meanings the participants construct around those lived experiences. That is, the third interview asks the respondents "how the factors in their lives interacted to bring them to their present situation. It also requires that they look at their present experience in detail and within the context in which it occurs" (pp. 18 – 19).

I adopted the structure of Seidman's (2006) three-interview series, but, in order that this project on 41 participants was manageable, I combined the three interviews on each participant into one. I designed an interview question sheet which contained three blocks of questions that tapped respectively a participant's (a) life contexts, such as educational and working experiences prior to coming to the university of focus, (b) concrete, detailed experiences with amalgamation, expansion, quality assurance policies and local innovations, (c) the meanings the participant attribute to their experiences. Among all, it was most important to "probe" the detailed examples, anecdotes and incidences on which opinions and attitudes were based. As I collapsed the three interview series with each participant into one, each interview lasted from 1.5 to 2 hours.

Interview techniques are important in minimizing the impact of the interviewer and the contexts on the interviewees. Yanow (2006) suggests that, although the researcher resigns from the role as an expert in the subject matter, he or she retains "process expertise, in knowing how to locate and access local knowledge and make it the subject of reflection, publicly discussable" (p. 23). I follow Seidman and others' guidelines through the interview process.

During each interview, after having asked the questions, I retreated to my "low-involvement" (Ochs & Capps, 2001) position, allowing the participants to develop and ramble on a topic as long as they like, as Atkinson (1998) and Seidman (2006) suggest, an interview is a chance for the participants, but not the researcher to talk.

There were moments when the participants were succinct and reserved, and refrained from providing vivid details of their experiences, partly because most of them, highly intellectual and well-educated, were used to stipulate their opinions along logico-scientific analytical line, but would not "degenerate" into the emotional, trivial and nagging telling of their lives. On such occasions, I would take over "tellership" by asking the participants to offer specific supporting examples, evidence, instances of the point they were making. For instance, "if expansion is detrimental to quality, did you ever experience specific instances that indicate that quality of education is declining?" "What routine tasks do you perform that are centrally controlled?" Seidman (2006) maintains that interviews are the reflections on past experiences, so that everything said in an interview may be called stories. Both Gabriel (1995) and Ochs and Capps (2001) suggest that stories are often not sole-authored, but are co-constructed by interlocutors in a conversation. For instance, Gabriel observed in his fieldwork that stories are often broached by one person who offers an element or two, and others contribute other elements to keep the story-telling going. According to Ochs and Capps, "tellership" shifts between two parties frequently; even if one of them assumes the position of a listener, he or she participates in construction by nodding, eye-contacting or inserting a comment to enable the telling to go on. I followed their suggestions and took part in the co-construction from time to time, albeit in a passive sense.

Thirty-two out of 41 interviews were tape recorded and later transcribed. Nine of the interviewees requested the tape-recorder to be turned off as I routinely consulted each of them if I could record the conversation. The presence of a tape recorder might unnerve and intimidate the participants, preventing them from providing factual details or raising controversial issues. They might give terse and less imaginative examples. In cases that I did not use a tape recorder, I committed the content I heard to paper or computer, immediately after the conversation. Recollection is regarded as a legitimate method by Gabriel (1998) in interviews involving life histories and vivid details, as he states that some contents "may be remembered years after the researcher first heard them and occasionally their meanings become clearer after one has assumed a certain emotional and time distance from the narrative" (p. 140).

Data analysis

The complete data set includes all the 32 interviews, and the written or typed recollections of the 9 interviews that I did not record. All interview notes and recorded interviews (after being transcribed) were translated into English and sent via e-mail to the participants for member check. Minor issues in translations were raised by several participants, for instance, one Professor of Mathematics corrected my translation of a few jargon terms in Mathematics.

The data I had were "qualitative in terms of texts" (Karlsson, 1993, p. 14). After several close readings of the entire data set, I tagged blocks of texts in which a participant was trying to make a point (or points) and assigned each block of text a number (which indicates the interviewee), a title and a short description or theme or summarizing phrase, a process Altheide (1987) called "qualitative content analysis" and Crabtree and Miller (1999) called "editing" form of organizing textual data. I cut each block of text with a number, title and theme out of its original transcripts, and pasted it into one excel document, which resulted in 588 blocks of texts to start with. Some examples of the blocks of texts with themes are "faculty members feel unqualified to teach unfamiliar subjects under the condition of expansion", "social science students' complain about lacking of resources after expansion", "preparation in students' text papers in teaching evaluation" "conflictual comments given by campus inspectors", etc.

In the second step, I tried to form assertions (Erickson, 1986) supported by texts of similar themes, while keeping open for "outliers" that disaffirm rather than confirm the emerging assertions. Both Erickson and Miles and Huberman (1994) maintain that the social world is complicated and non-unitary, so that finding rivalry evidence or "outliers" is necessary in order to qualify the emerging explanations and theories. They both maintain that if the researchers obtain too perfect, overwhelming and one-directional data, there probably is something wrong in either the collection or analysis process, and researchers need to go back and check.

So in this second step, I did two things. First, was to group confirming and disaffirming data bits (text blocks with themes) into different categories. Second, was to compare the different experiences within and across groups. For instance, all students' experiences and faculty members' experiences were grouped respectively into two categories, and through comparison of different experiences among faculty members and students respectively, the disparities in social-sciences/humanities and natural sciences/technological disciplines gradually emerge. Likewise, I grouped faculty members' experiences with the national teaching evaluations together. By comparing faculty members' members' experiences, the differential power between senior academics and junior academics emerged, and by comparing academics with administrators, the difference in attitudes and responses emerged. It was through this merging and comparison process, that the assertions gradually come into being.

While generating the assertions, I kept looking for disconfirming data that can qualify the assertions. For instance, in the experiences of expansion, while criticisms were dominating, there were also contradictory voices on the benefits of the expansion. Likewise, some faculty members members viewed the national teaching evaluation in a positive light, while others referred to it as "formalistic through and through". In this second step, I generated assertions, through merging and comparing data bits and deliberately finding contrary and disconfirming data bits to quality these assertions. I present the assertions in chapters 4 to 6.

Chapter 4

University People's Experiences and Perceptions of the Amalgamation and Expansion Polices

I have outlined in Chapter 2, the Literature Review section that the grand narratives of national HE reform policies, amalgamation and expansion, are constructed along the line of neoliberal economic rationality, the quest for economic efficiency and return. The amalgamation policy is vested with the hope of achieving efficient distribution of scarce resources among universities, while the expansion policy is predicated on the premise that universities are engines of national economy and international competition.

In this chapter, I examine how distant national HE reform policies are experienced, reconstituted or resisted by university people in their day to day practices. Rich and detailed empirical evidence is displayed on how front-line faculty members, administrators and students perceive and respond to, and how they read different and opposite meanings off, the amalgamation and expansion policies, as Trowler (2001) comments that "policy discourse can be understood as polysemic 'text' amenable to alternative readings at variance with that encoded by policy-makers" (p. 184). I present the assertions, qualified by both confirming and disconfirming data bits (blocks of texts with themes) derived from data analysis (see Chapter 3 for more detailed descriptions of data analysis).

▶ Chapter 4　University People's Experiences and Perceptions of the Amalgamation and Expansion Polices

Experiences with and Resistance to the Amalgamation Policy

In the officially sanctioned discourses, amalgamation brings about internal and external efficiency through merging and integrating different institutions. The university of focus merged with a medical college, a traffic junior college and a geological secondary vocational school in 2000, which were all geographically adjacent to the university of focus. This type of amalgamation is called "acquisition", as the weaker institutions are absorbed by or dissolved into the stronger, master university. The interviews at the university of focus suggest that the merger occurred at the physical rather than discursive or cultural level. For instance, the Admission Offices of different institutions collapsed into one central Admission Office, with the responsibility and tasks redistributed and reallocated among all staff members. However, according to the interviews conducted at the university of focus, the boundaries of the pre-amalgamation institutions are reinforced rather than weakened or dissolving after 8 years of amalgamation. University people tend to stress their former group affiliations and "otherize" their current colleagues in the interviews. There is a cliquish, conflictual and confrontational air between groups defined by their former institutional afflications, which reminds me of Argyris' (1993) humorous rendering of people's attitudes in a conflictual situation in an organization: If you do not bother me, I will not bother you. If you have cancer, I will probably speak to you. Such group confrontation creates winners and losers. There are certain social groups that are marginalized and victimized, taking the blame for declining university reputation, decreased bonus payouts, etc. Resistance to the official macro-story on amalgamation proliferates at the local level.

Experiences with amalgamation

The "old" faculty members at the flagship university of focus and the "new" faculty members from other smaller institutions project hostility and aloofness onto each other. At best, they adopt the rule of mutual non-interference with regard to each other's affairs. The worse case is that the "old" faculty members, implicitly and explicitly, tend to marginalize and victimize the "new" faculty members.

Mutual non-interference. Professor Qing in the Department of Mathematics remarks that "I do not know what they are doing".

> As I belong to the original "core" of this flagship university, and excel in teaching and research, I do not feel that I am affected at all by the amalgamation. I do not know what "they" are doing. I mean, those faculty members from the Geological Vocational Secondary School. They might be having a difficult time, but frankly I do not know. I guess it is hard for them, as before they are teaching in secondary schools, but now they have to adapt to the university environment. It is normal if they are laid off, as they do not have the professional credentials to be here.

Professor Tao, Associate Dean of the College of Humanities, is more sensitive to the engulfment that exists between the "old" and "new" faculty members. She comments that

> Although the amalgamation took place a long time ago—it has been 8 years—I feel that we are not well integrated. The original faculty members at this university and those from other institutions have different psychologies. They have gap in qualities. We must admit it. A university like ours has very high expectations for

faculty members. However, faculty members from the junior college and the secondary school are limited in their abilities. We must admit this. After so many years of adapting to each other, we are gradually closing up the gap. The gap still exists, though. While in talking, we always talk about "they who are from other institutions" and "we who are from this institution". There are such differences. The gap between psychologies and ideas is indeed difficult to bridge. Everyone is feeling that he or she is deprived of something in the amalgamation.

According to Professor Zhu, a former faculty member of the Medical College who came to work at the university of focus after amalgamation, it is her own choice to stay aloof, which echoes the concept of "hollowed collegiality" (Dill, 2003; Massy, Wilger, Colbeck, 1994). Her remarks are

> I feel awkward with the social network... It was really awful at the beginning. As faculty members our social relations are simple. I go home after finishing teaching the classes. I stay at home for days when I do not have to teach. There is little contact between me and my colleagues. We do not communicate a lot. I am only on nodding terms with those "old" faculty members at this university. We greet and walk by. We do not interact a lot. Those "old" faculty members at this university have known each other for a long time. They know well each other's families. They are deeply attached to each other, while I have difficulty being integrated into this collectivity. I am feeling this way. I would rather stay at home than coming to the university. I will show up when there are compulsory faculty meetings. This is the direct impact of the amalgamation on us. It is not their fault.

> They have worked together for many years. It is not necessary for them to incorporate me. I choose to stay at a distance.

Marginalization and victimization of the "new" faculty members. It is likely that the "old" faculty members and administrators marginalize and victimize the "new" faculty members and administrators, blaming them for lacking professional training, tarnishing the university's reputation, lowering bonus payouts, and being bureaucratic. The interviews on the "new" faculty members from the other institutions, on the contrary, focus on the worsened working conditions and salaries in post-amalgmation conditions.

Professor Wei from the Department of Politics and Administration is blaming faculty members from other institutions for complicating the "pure composition" of faculty members in the department. In the current wave of university development, all faculty members without terminal degrees are obliged to enter doctoral programs. Although most faculty members, "old" or "new", are equally undergraduate degree holders, Professor Wei hints that "old" faculty members are better positioned to obtain higher degrees than "new" faculty members from other institutions. Because of the presence of "them," the department's goal of improving educational attainments of all its faculty force is unattainable. She makes long comments that

> Before the amalgamation, the composition of our faculty members is very pure. All of us are from formal, flagship institutions, because this university only recruits graduates from flagship institutions. So the original faculty members in our college have very strong undergraduate education. Although we have strong undergraduate education, as we graduated in early 80s, few of us pursue Master's degrees. We were allocated to different posts by

the State immediately after graduation. We were just concerned with earning humble salaries, but not engaging ourselves in research. We did not do much research, but only taught students. Many years have passed. Suddenly, we found that we were out of date. We have to elevate ourselves, by pursuing doctoral degrees. Because we have very strong undergraduate education, we would not have problems with pursuing doctoral studies. In China, the policy goes that if you have already obtained associate professor's rank, you can enter a doctoral program without undertaking Master's study. I do not know if this applies in the United States. As most of us have obtained the rank of associate professor, we are eligible to enter doctoral studies.

Professor Wei continues to emphasize that "new" faculty members are less qualified than the "old" faculty members in terms of educational backgrounds, experiences, which in some way limits the department's scope of development.

After amalgamating other three institutions which are of low-status, our faculty members' backgrounds are very diverse, in terms of knowledge and disciplines. Under such condition, it is unrealistic to try to push all our faculty members to pursue doctoral degrees. Some of the faculty members from the other institutions are quite old; it is difficult for them to pursue doctoral studies. So we change our slogan to "eliminate bachelors". We encourage faculty members with only undergraduate degrees to obtain at least Master's degrees. The faculty members from those smaller institutions are not like us. Although we only have undergraduate degrees, our undergraduate backgrounds are strong. We've obtained associate professor's rank, so we are eligible to apply for doctoral programs. They, even though older than us, are not eligible to apply for doctoral programs, so entering Master's programs might be sufficient for them.

Mr. Bai in the Office of Disciplinary Development, attributes the university's lowered place in the reputation rank to the "new" faculty members from other institutions. "It is their poor quality that drags the university down"—it is a prevailing view, aired by faculty members, administrators and students as well. Mr. Bai reasons that

> If a person has stayed in a certain environment for a long time, he or she will be socialized into certain habits and behaviors. So the original faculty members at this university are broad-mined and inspired… in terms of ideas and management… The faculty members from the Traffic Junior College and Geological Vocational Secondary School do not realize this. They are passive and confined. The university is sliding down in the reputational rank. The amalgamation is detrimental to us, because those ineligible faculty members are filling up the positions in the departments and colleges. There are no position openings, so that the university is not able to recruit more qualified faculty members. The quality of faculty force is the essence and soul of the university. Our university's reputation is declining, and it is declining very fast.

Professor's Su's opinion is that, after amalgamation, the departmental income is divided by more people so that it means diminishing bonus payouts. He states that

> We used to be a small unit, with around 18 faculty members. We used to divide the income [from a for-profit training program] among ourselves. In 1999, we

each received a laptop as bonus ... After 2000, our faculty members were more than doubled. There are 30 to 40 people in the department ... We no longer have generous bonus payouts for the Labors' day, or the National day. Now there are more monks, but the porridge does not increase.

Mr. Dou is the Vice Director of the university's Office of Public Relations. He sees that administrators from smaller institutions are more "bureaucratic" than those from a flagship university. He tells the following story.

> The cultures and traditions of a certain university influence the individuals; those administrators have a small-institution mentality. For instance, a small institution will create various impediments for a faculty member who wants to further study, as the institution is striving to retain personnel. So their administrators tend to "manage" people. Our university always encourages individual development and the free flow of talents. So we are more open and flexible. I am indigenous to this university. I graduated from this university, and have worked in several offices and units ever since. I know that we are "serving" the university while those administrators from small institutions try to control and manipulate other people.

"New" faculty members' responses to the amalgamation. The "new" faculty members and administrators from other institutions provide their perspectives in response to the tales that marginalize and victimize them. In general, former administrators from those smaller institutions are more satisfied with the amalgamation, which is consistent with the research conducted by Q. Wang & J. Lin (2005). For instance, Mr. Kong, Director of the Subunit of Teaching Evaluation and Mr. You, Director of the Office of Student Affairs, refer to themselves as the beneficiaries of the amalgamation policy. Both of them keep positions at the flagship university which are parallel to their positions in the smaller institutions, which to them is an elevation of social status. Mr. You even describes himself as "being hit by a pancake falling down from the sky." In contrast, some of the "new" faculty members passively internalize what is said about them. Some, comparing the pre- and post-amalgamation conditions, condemn the amalgamation as an uncontrollable, hegemonic process imposed on helpless individuals. Still some others describe the way they strive to adapt and integrate to the social world of the flagship university.

Professor Han lamented that amalgamation altered permanently her easy life-style, as top-down policies are given to the individuals and are uncontrollable. She has to cope with much lower pay and heavier workload, while taking on various blames. All she wants to do is to keep the job.

> We [the traffic junior college] located at the center of the city. We rented out part of our campus for commercial purposes...we were much better off before the amalgamation. Some revenue from renting out our property turned into our bonus payouts. Our pay was 2 to 3 times more than what we receive now. After coming to this flagship university, our pay is significantly lowered. I am feeling out of place too. I have difficulty relating to professors at this flagship university as colleagues. Now, I only hope that I will not be laid off. I never again think of promotion. The flagship university is happy to swallow our land and facilities; I guess they are not happy to take us in.

There are "striving-to-adapt" stories aired by Professor Zhu in

▶ Chapter 4 University People's Experiences and Perceptions of the Amalgamation and Expansion Polices

the School of Law. Life after amalgamation to her is an endless chasing of higher degrees against all types of impediments. Her description of the life after amalgamation is that

> Most of the faculty members from the Medical College and the Traffic Junior College have only undergraduate degrees. The "old" faculty members at this flagship university are at least Master's. We have different starting points. The university policy had that, in 2002, only Master's or higher degree holders could teach. We felt enormous pressure. Most of us rushed into Master's programs. Then, after a few years, we feel the dire need to obtain doctoral degrees. It is not university policy, but it is radically pushed in our school. The pressure is very real on me. When doctoral degree is not required, I just feel a little uncomfortable among those who are terminal degree holders. Now our school makes it very explicit that doctoral degree is a must. The fear is very tangible. They set the limit that if I do not obtain a doctoral degree in 5 years, I will be out of the scene… Again, all of us try to rush into doctoral programs.

Professor Zhu tells me that she has to make hard choices between work and family after amalgamation. Although she manages to stick to her current position, there are many who are forced out of their jobs because of the post-amalgamation pressure and rising standards.

> I was considering taking another job, or being a stay-at-home mom. I think if I work another job, I do not have to obtain the doctoral degree. I work and go home. I am free to control the time after work. But the doctoral coursework has no limit. I have to contribute to it day and night, at home and school. There is no limit. I am tired.

I talked about this to everyone I know. They told me that if I did switch to an administrative, supporting-staff position, it is equally tiring. They advised me not giving up my current job. At this university, a faculty member can switch to a staff's position, but a staff cannot be turned into a faculty member. This is a one way road… So I hesitated. They told me: "You are still young. Muster all your courage and resources and obtain the degree!" If I am still twenty something… Those faculty members who are older than me… They are also pursuing their doctoral degrees. The current situation is that, all the faculty members in the law school are pursuing doctoral degrees.

In short, the heated group competitions and conflicts create winners and losers. There is a considerable degree of marginalization and victimization of faculty members and administrators from the smaller institutions with which the flagship university of focus merged. The amalgamation policy, implemented top-down through administrative fiat, is based on the rationale of economic efficiency. The valuable, scarce resources of the smaller institutions (e.g., land and facilities) are taken over by the flagship university. While all faculty members and administrators equally experience lowering pay, worsening working conditions, deteriorating reputation, and more social conflicts and confrontations after the amalgamation, the "new" faculty members are taking on most of the blames. The situation is, as Professor Qing describes, "Everyone is feeling that he or she is deprived of something in the amalgamation".

Resistance to the amalgamation

There are some people that reaffirm the official storyline on improving internal efficiency through amalgamation. For instance,

▶ Chapter 4   University People's Experiences and Perceptions of the Amalgamation and Expansion Polices

Sheng, a doctoral student in the Department of Chemistry, stresses the importance of sharing resources through amalgamation. He says that

> In the discipline of chemistry, we had a new concentration, medicine. Because they bring their research in medicine here… Our research is more systematic. In our area… the equipment is expensive. Strong as our university is, it is impossible for the university to buy all the equipment. Even if we buy all the equipment, it will be outdated in two years. It is just like the computer that is updated very fast. The old equipment will not function well, and yield inaccurate data. If we amalgamate with another institution that brings us equipment, we can share the resources.

There are strong voices that resist the amalgamation. Apart from focusing on the group competitions and confrontations that create winners and losers, the university people air views and opinions on what "ideal" institutions should be like. According to Professor He, the Associate Dean of the Law School, a gigantic organization outstretching itself means low efficiency, more attritions and longer waiting time in work.

> Amalgamation is influencing us greatly. The so called super university is composed of blocks of units. The integration of those blocks is full of struggles. The integration of administrative units is very complicated. Now after the integration of the administrative units, it is very difficult to get something done. For instance, if you want to process some documents, now you have to obtain two official stamps instead of one. It consumes our energy and time… How could academics benefit from it?

Professor He emphasizes that he prefers a small institution, as the one he visited in Swiss right before he started to work at the current university. He asserts that

> Before I came to work at this university, I was a visiting scholar at a small and cozy institution in Swiss. The idea that a larger institution is better is alien in foreign counties. Stanford University is an example. It is very small but prestigious. The idea that the amalgamation brings more efficiency is just a myth. It is a political slogan. All universities get excited and want to merge with each other but they do not know what they are really doing. They are like a flock of sheep, blindly following the leader sheep. If you ask me what amalgamation means to me, it just means more managerial units. You have to deal with more upper-level administrative units in your work.

A president that resists top-down fiat on merger is regarded as a hero. There are rumors that the university of focus and another flagship university in the city will merge. The rumors came around in late 1990s, but died down soon. A new round of rumors prevailed around 2005. Such talking on the merger of two flagship universities never turns into reality, which many university people attribute to their heroic deceased university president. According to Mohrman's (2003) observation, Chinese university presidents seldom act with autonomy; they maintain close ties with governmental officials, and will take actions only after having obtained sanctions or acquiesce from the top political leaders. Any president who successfully resists top-down fiats will be regarded as a hero, regardless of what the president is resisting. The comments made by Wu, a sophomore student in the Department of Radio Engineering, echoes what Mohrman states about people's attitudes towards a defiant and incompliant university president.

> ... But this request [on the amalgamation of two

► Chapter 4   University People's Experiences and Perceptions of the Amalgamation and Expansion Polices

flagship universities] was declined by our late president. He delivered several public speeches on this. He said that amalgamation does not make a first-tier university. A university should develop through self-renewal. Amalgamation elevates a university's position in the ranking list, but it does not improve the university's inner strength. A university needs to accumulate tradition and culture to develop. But the amalgamation does not serve this purpose. Among students, some of us would like to see such amalgamation ... The proposal is turned down by the [late] president. We still all regard him as our hero.

Some interviews on faculty members, administrators and students suggest that, the Medical School remains intact and impenetrable in the compelling discourses of merger and integration. The Medical School used to be the core, central unit of the Medical College that the university of focus acquired in 2000. Although all the other departments and units in the Medical College (which was in actuality a comprehensive university) were torn apart and integrated into the university of focus, the Medical School is resistant and incompliant, which sometimes is achieved through subtle and manipulative strategies. For instances, although it is quite common for undergraduates to switch majors, according to Hua and Jin, two seniors in the Medical School, curricula are subtlety manipulated so that the free flow of students between the Medical School and the other parts of the university are blocked. Their comments go like that

Some students in our school want to switch majors. However, the school wants to retain students. It prevents students from leaving by manipulating the curricula. For instance, the mathematics in our school was too simple for most of the other majors. If students want to take the

Advanced Mathematics A from other departments, they need to give up their own courses in our own school. It is quite risky for us to skip core courses in our own major. They deliberately make the schedule difficult for the students to take classes from other departments. So it is almost impossible for students in the school to switch to other majors.

Furthermore, Mr. Qi, Secretary General in the Department of Bioscience and Medical Engineering, tells a story about how the Medical School successfully resists the supervision of the university-level Overseeing and Guiding (*Dudao*) Team. Since 1989, the university's Office of Teaching Affairs started to invite senior and retired professors to form the *Dudao* Team, to randomly observe, evaluate and suggest on young (under the age of 40) faculty members' classes. In 1993, the university started to sponsor annual teaching contests among voluntary participating young faculty members, with the same team members serving as judges at the contests. In short, the *Dudao* Team is a deeply-entrenched local quality-assurance mechanism in which one centralized team is in charge of observing and advising on teaching practices across the university (more detailed information on the *Dudao* Team will be provided in Chapter 5). The Medical School, however, is resistant towards the centralized team. Mr. Qi comments that

> In teaching and research, we are minding our own business. There isn't real integration. Although the Medical School is part of the university now, we have our own supervisors. We are more experienced in supervising our own teaching, as our discipline has its own logic. I like the situation better at Zhejiang University. Their scale is very large. Last time, the teaching supervisors of Zhejiang University visited us. They are a gigantic team.

> Chapter 4　University People's Experiences and Perceptions of the Amalgamation and Expansion Polices

> I asked them if their team has a leader, they said no. Each campus has its own team and leader. We like it better if we do not have to answer to others at the university, as we are an independent discipline.

In short, social conflicts and confrontations exist on the post-amalgamation campus, with a particular social group, the "new" faculty members from the smaller institutions, marginalized and victimized. This group is blamed for lowering bonus payouts, lacking professional credentials and tarnishing the university's reputation, while this group simultaneously offers counter stories on striving to adapt to the social world of the flagship university.

Furthermore, views and opinions that counter the official rationales of the amalgamation prevail at the university of focus. There are parodies of the official grand narratives, stating that amalgamation results in inefficiency instead of efficiency. There are stories that enthusiastically recount the president's resistance to amalgamation, and deem such resistance, almost blindly, as heroic. Furthermore, the interviews reveal that amalgamated units remain intact and impenetrable, sometimes through subtle and manipulative strategies. Resistance to the amalgamation proliferates at the university of focus.

Experiences with and Perceptions of the Expansion Policy

The analysis on the interviews with students and faculty members reveals that students are mostly concerned with educational quality, and faculty members with working conditions on the post-expansion campus. Students and faculty members not only reflect upon how they experience the expansion policy (what is), but also constantly make the "normative leap", articulating what ought to be. Social justice issues, attracting most attention from students and faculty members, are regarded as the utmost impediment to the continuing enforcement of the expansion policy. Another issue emerges from the analysis is the disparate and contrastive treatment of natural sciences/technological disciplines and social sciences/humanities disciplines in the expansion.

Students' experiences with the expansion

Some students and faculty members deem the expansion policy as enabling widening access. Undergraduate students are complaining that the quality of their education is deteriorating because of large class sizes as well as decreased student-faculty interactions. In retrospection of his undergraduate education, Wang, the first-year Master's student in the School of Economics and Management, thinks that education at the university of focus is not different from high schools, as class size prohibits more conducive activities like small group discussions and collaborative projects. He expects his courses in economic theories to be smaller and inquiry-based, with the instructor playing a facilitator role in constructive conversations. His comments are that

> The professors and instructors focus on teaching seminars, while I think that our education should be more research based.... We are just acquiring knowledge from the books... Last time, when my professor went to attend a conference on e-commerce in Hong Kong, he told me that many undergrads from Taiwan were attending. However, we were not having any such chances; we were just reading the news about them. Even I am a graduate student now, I am still having high-school mode of education. Although at present time, we have more interactions with professors, and are gradually learning to think independently. At undergraduate level, professors just fed facts into our brain. For instance, in the economic theory course, we just memorized different

theories. We seldom were encouraged to critique each theory, or to apply the theory to real life situations.

In resonance with him, Li, a sophomore student in the Department of Politics and Administration, speaks about her experience of having to cope with the meager resources on the new campus, built in 2006 to accommodate the rapidly expanding student body. She says that

> I feel that we are pioneers on the new campus... There were bricks and tiles everywhere. The dormitories were just built. Our library was open last winter, in the January of 2007. Before that, we couldn't obtain any materials. We did not have internet connection in the dormitory then. We could not surf online. The public computer room was stuffed with people. Now our environment is improving a little. There are internet bars you can use once for a while. Before, within a radius of 5 *li*, there was scarcely anyone there. It was not convenient for teachers to commute to this campus.

To Li, the real experiences on campus are vastly different from what she heard from older students,

> Before, older students told me that they had a lot of chances to interact with professors. But now, there are few chances of such interactions. The professors, in the morning strive to come here on time. After classes, they, carrying their bags, run off very quickly. So, the facilities for living and other activities might be ok in this region... in terms of the software—as it is a technological institution, they build labs more advanced than elsewhere—they do not focus on building facilities for social sciences. The books we have in the library are very few.

Zheng, a doctoral student in the Department of Philosophy and Science, has experienced three HE institutions, another university in the same city (pseudonym SNU), Yunnan University and the current university. He compares his pre-expansion experiences at SNU 15 years ago with his current education,

> ... I was at SNU 15 years ago. I felt that at that time, I was cared about as a person. Every Monday, our head teacher (*banzhuren*) would teach us politics and ethics. He/she would ask us how our life and study was. He/she inquired about my study process. He/she asked each of us, how many living expenses we were having each month. If we were having financial difficulties, he/she would help us apply for students' aids. In the winter, each of us got a cotton-stuffed coat from the school. He/she cared more about students who were from rural areas, who were living in poverty. He/she helped not only my studies, but my life. At SNU, each undergraduate class had one head teacher.

Zheng is quite critical towards the universities he attended later, emphasizing that, in the context of expansion, apart from deterioration of academic services, there is a lack of humanitarian care. As he specializes in Chinese philosophy, he advocates an idealized version of mentor-student relationship with more "humanitarian care" in the university setting. But the fact is that there is a shortage of staff. He says that

> ... the universities I attended later, including Yunnan University and the current University... As long as you have done your thesis/dissertation, you can do. Especially on this new campus, professors disappear immediately after they have taught the classes. There is little professor-student interaction. Now, one head

teacher is in charge of many classes, because the university is pursuing economic efficiency. One head teacher is in charge of the whole grade. In this way, students seldom communicate with the teachers. I mean the undergraduate students. Yunnan University is the same.

Wu, an undergraduate in the Department of Radio Engineering, sees that he is prevented from exercising consumer rights under the condition of expansion. He feels obliged to evaluate faculty members positively. As faculty members are already overloaded with work, it won't improve anyone's work if he rates any faculty members negatively, but only gets himself into trouble. His story is that

> The professors believe in this: If a class rates a faculty member very low, then the students in that class have problems. These students must be lazy. For instance, in the Department of Electronic Engineering, there was a mathematics instructor that was not liked by the students. Students felt that the instruction work was poor, and they did not do well in the tests. Later, we heard from the departmental and university leaders, that the students in this class were not hard working. They did not spend time in the materials, which resulted in their poor performance in the tests. But the students attributed their poor performance to the instructor ... The departmental and university leaders will try to persuade us that the instructor might be partially responsible, but we'd better spend more time looking at the inadequacy in ourselves rather than blaming the instructor...

Wu continues to describe that sometimes very subtle and manipulative measures will be taken by the university personnel to prevent students from raising controversial issues and exasperating the already intense employer-employee relations at the university of focus.

Sometimes our counselor (*fudaoyuan*) will advise us that if we evaluate an instructor low, the instructor will be mad. As at a university, the instructor controls students' grades, the poor evaluation will lower the whole class' grades. If the students affirm the instructor's teaching, he/she will be in a good mood and will be more devoted to teaching. So our counselor hopes that we are more affirmative towards the instructors. Sometimes, when we are filling out the teaching evaluation forms, or are voting for our favorite instructors, our counselor will watch us closely.

Faculty members' experiences with the expansion

Faculty members' experiences with the expansion, just as students', seldom fall within the contour of the official storyline on the prosperity and economic gains through expansion. Faculty members' stories center on increased and more challenging work with lowering pay. With expansion, the increase of enrolmnents exceeds the expansion of faculty force by 2 to 3 times. Faculty members are forced to change life style, cope with unfamiliar subjects and face changing and diverse student body.

To many faculty members, having to commute to the new campus, built to cater to the vastly expanded student body, upsets their familiar, comfortable state of being. Many feel that they have difficulty juggling different tasks on different campuses. Shi, associate professor in the Department of Mathematics, complained about having to commute between different campuses.

Before, we have a lot of communications with the

students. Even if I am not in the office, the students can find me at home. Now, how can they find me? Is it possible that I run to the new campus upon students' request? It takes me 50 minutes to ride in a taxi, and I will be worried about how I can come back home. It might not be my individual case. I live in the city, and my child is very young. I guess most faculty members are like me. We have to catch the bus. I leave the classroom the moment the bell rings, because the bus to the city is leaving in 15 minutes. I do not talk to students after classes, unless they need me for something in particular. It is because we do not have to stay in our offices.

For Professor Wei in the Department of Politics and Administration, expansion means that faculty members have to teach subjects in unfamiliar areas.

They [the university] build all the majors that are attractive to the students, but don't care if there are the faculty members for such majors. They are allocating teaching tasks to faculty members who have never learned such areas before. Some faculty members are conscientious, willing to spend time on a topic they have never taught before. Some faculty members might not know the subjects themselves before they come to the classroom. They are quite brave. This has negative consequences on teaching quality. The deterioration is caused by the expansion. There are not enough investments in HE, and the increase of faculty force is not commensurate with the increase of students. I was caught in such a situation … I was not teaching what I am specializing in. When the department head said to me, "teach this course please", I answered, "all right, I will teach it." If you are diligent enough, you will learn while teaching. For most of the faculty members, they do not know what they are teaching.

For most faculty members, the challenge in work under the condition of expansion comes from the changing and mixed student body. Professor Xu's story reveals that the overall quality of student body is declining while Professor Cao, who is in charge of engineering students' internships and experiments, views students' composition as more diverse and mixed. Xu's said that

> Each year, the undergraduate students I am supervising are of poorer and poorer quality. I mean they are doing poor in their graduation projects. In the technological department, students must complete practical projects to graduate. The teacher assigns them tasks, and they design. But they are poor in it. I think those students should not be studying in undergraduate programs here. According to their abilities—as people have different abilities—they must be in much less demanding programs. We have to assign them easier projects, in accordance to their abilities. We do not insist on high standards anymore.

Cao's story, in contrast with Xu's, focuses on the diversity of student population. He said that

> Now we enroll around 30,000 undergrads. In general, the quality of students declined... many people who do not have chances to be educated before are educated now. For instance, many children in the rural area are able to enter colleges... The college entrance examination is one high-stakes test that determines a person's whole life. In the rural high schools, some students never had experiences with experiments, as their

▶ Chapter 4   University People's Experiences and Perceptions of the Amalgamation and Expansion Polices

schools do not have good facilities. But the graduates from the urban areas are well aquatinted with experiments. In terms of scores, the students from rural areas might have higher scores. When they are educated at the same time, I do not expect to teach them on the basis of their scores in the entrance examination. Some of them need extra education, in order that the teaching of experiment can be carried on. This is another problem I face with expansion... Compared to the students before the expansion, our current students are more diverse and mixed. In terms of education, I have to differentiate the students and educate them in accordance to their personal abilities. We need to think about how to educate the individual students.

Despite the fact that their working conditions become more challenging, complex and uncertain in the context of expansion, most faculty members find that they are not compensated by better salaries. In contrast, their salaries lower. Such stories are typically articulated by faculty members in those disciplines where alternative channels of incomes (e. g., funding and part-time jobs) are more limited. Professor Han says that

Now at our university, we receive relative lower pay among all colleges/universities in this city... It is because the new campus is using much of our resources. Faculty pay is dragged down by the building of the new campus. It is natural. It is like a family. If a family is building a new house, it will not be able to afford new clothes for you. You have to do without them, since the current clothes are not too old or too ragged. If the family is not building the house, it will afford new clothes for you. Now, it cannot afford them.

Resistance to the expansion policy

When questioned on their perceptions of the future of the expansion policy, most interview participants in the sample of this study offer versions of stories on "what ought to be". As the opinions and views they constructed contradict the official encoding of the expansion policy, I call these stories "resistance." Among all resistance stories, the concern for social justice emerges as a most salient issue.

Professor Qing in the Department of Mathematics sees expansion policy as myopic, focusing on short- but not long-term economic gains. He anticipates diseconomy in the future. He says that

> In China, this is a particular period. There are many people that are between 15 and 25. These people need to be educated. The state is trying to expand higher education to cater to their needs. Between 1999 and now, the whole educational system has been expanding radically. Many new campuses are built. But the birth rate of Chinese people is dropping. In 10 years, the people who want to enter the universities will drop, be fewer than the enrolments now. At that time, universities will be facing low enrolments. The many campuses we built now will be deserted.

More faculty members and students are focusing on the tuition paying system that pushes away many excellent students; financial conditions become an embedded pre-requisite for college entrance. Thus, eliminating financial disparities is deemed the chief priority. Professor Tao, Associate Dean of College of Humanities, remarks that

> Most prestigious universities are charging higher

fees. Some universities did not charge tuitions, but the good universities, like Beijing, Qinghua, Fudan and Nanjing Universities started experimenting cost-sharing a long time ago. Some students, constrained by money, prefer to enter those ordinary universities that do not charge fees. Still some other students who do enter our program are leading a hard time. As their advisor, I am empathetic towards them. I will try to provide them with some chances of research, so that they can earn some money. Some of them have to work part time to support themselves. I have to allow them to take part-time jobs.

Cao continues to analyze that social justice is the chief reason that the expansion policy is forced out of place,

Expansion is detrimental to those students from poor families. Many more students are entering universities, but for certain groups of students, the expansion means that they lose the chance for ever. I know that expansion will be stopped soon, not because that there are many more students than the university can cater to, but because there are too many students who are left out of HE in the context of expansion.

In a similar fashion as Professor Tao, Yun, a doctoral student, sees that expansion will not be continuously implemented, due to the cost-sharing policy that is embedded in it. As anger and resistance accumulate, the policy has to come to a halt. He makes calculations on the financial difficulty rural students encounter, which to him is the greatest impediment to the implementation of expansion policy.

Expansion will not last long. I tell you; it won't. Some people are happy with but some others are upset by it. The State is thinking about increasing revenues

> through undergraduate expansion... I will give an example of my neighbor. In rural areas, the income from two *mu* of fields is meager. Now the price of grain is 7 *mao* per *jin*. The income from one *mu* of field is around ￥700 to ￥800 yuan. The income from selling the grain is very, very little, subtracted by the costs of fertilizer and pesticides. The tuitions students have to pay are too high for such a family. Even though the elementary and middle schools in rural areas are free, parents cannot afford the fees for books and students' living expenses. Parents will not regard entering college as a possibility for students. They will prefer their children to drop out and take up part-time jobs, regardless if their children are boys or girls.

Yun further stresses that the inaccessible tuitions are compounded by the limited coverage of students' aids. Application of students' aids is complicated by personal network (*guanxi*) on campus. He says that

> It depends on your personal network (*guanxi*) to apply for students' aids. You have to be a pet student of your professors... At this university, like in other places, a teacher will help their favorite students get students' aids. Last semester, a student applied for students' aids, and received ￥1,000 to ￥2,000 yuan per semester. Now he spent all the money on a cell phone. I do not think that he is really needy. Really poor students might not be able to access students' aids, while rich students can.

The story Professor Shi tells is related to teaching quality. There is no incentive to improve teaching quality under the current condition that every faculty member is working overtime. He depicts the ideal situation in which the number of academics is surplus in relation to that of students, and in which each faculty member is motivated to improve the quality of their work.

In theory, students have chances to pick the instructors. Students and faculty members are mutually selecting each other. However, I feel that this is not realizable under the current conditions. Take the course I am teaching as an example. We have all together five instructors, but we've got to teach eight classes. Do you think it realistic to ask students to choose the instructors? The purpose of the system is that, excellent instructors will be favored by students. That is, more students will be enrolling in their classes, so that there are distances between excellent and bad instructors. The bad instructors will be prompted to make progress. However, the reality is, five instructors are teaching eight classes. It is not possible for anyone of us to be assigned to the waiting bench. This is a false system, not realizing its own goals. There is no incentive for the instructors.

According to Shi, university instructors should be more competitive among themselves, so that "improvement" might be their focus.

To improve teaching quality, there should be incentive for faculty members. If there are nine instructors for eight classes, one of them must be assigned to the waiting bench. During the time he/she is waiting, he/she might seek to improve him/herself. This is significant. Now we have three classes that do not have instructors. We instructors are overloaded with teaching, and we have to teach more than necessary. The system is just false; it is not giving the chance for instructors to improve themselves.

In short, there are multiple views and opinions that resist the official accounts on the profit-making expansion policy. There are stories on diseconomy, social inequality, and poor teaching quality. This suggests that instead of working straight with the university people, the official grand narratives on economic rationality encounter multiple contending and competing readings of the policy that grow out of the day-to-day social interactions in the local setting.

Disparities between disciplines under the expansion conditions

Another salient issue that emerges through the analysis of the interviews on the expansion policy is the disparate and differential treatment of natural sciences/technological disciplines and social sciences/humanities disciplines. The former disciplines are more favorably and strategically located in national grand narratives on economic development and international integration, and in institutional traditions. Under expansion conditions, although resources are stringent for all disciplines, funding priorities are given to natural sciences and technologies disciplines. Furthermore, due to the fallacy and pitfalls in university admission policy, some social sciences and humanities units are shrinking and struggling with retention issues, against a backdrop of 5-time increase in undergraduate enrolments in 8 years.

The natural sciences and technologies disciplines thrive on national policies of "revitalizing the nation through science and education" which is predicated on the assumption that "science and technology are productivity" (J. L. Wu & Fan, 2007; R. S. Gao, 2007). Furthermore, in China's preoccupation with gaining parity or even leadership in the world's knowledge system, more resources and funding are directed towards disciplines that are more likely to

▶ Chapter 4 University People's Experiences and Perceptions of the Amalgamation and Expansion Polices

be integrated into the Western-oriented sciences and higher education (Altbach, 2001). In other words, national policies are targeting natural, engineering and biomedical sciences for specific development and intensive investments, given their likelihood of acquiring international recognition (e. g., publishing in international renowned journals) while leaving other areas, mostly indigenous humanities and social sciences, to their own devices (R. Yang, 2004).

The institutional history and tradition as a technological institution are confounding with the national policy environment and serve to further marginalize social sciences and humanities disciplines, which were more recently created and established in the late 1980s. Most participants in social sciences and humanities disciplines in this study raise the issue that most of the university leaders who are "technological majors themselves," do not understand the idiosyncrasies of social sciences and humanities disciplines and think that these disciplines do not need investments.

Fund allocation under the expansion conditions. Although the university has built the first-rate labs and equipment for the natural sciences and technologies majors, there are very limited library resources for humanities and social sciences disciplines. Not only are there few books in the library, but also channels to obtain materials elsewhere are blocked. According to Professor Kong, a high-ranked university administrator, 70% of the first disbursement of "985" grant went to building infrastructure (e. g., building labs and purchasing equipment) for natural sciences and technological disciplines. Stories about the lack of resources for humanities and social sciences disciplines proliferate. Professor He complains about the scarcity of books in the library.

> .... When I go to the library, there are very few books on humanities and social sciences ... Before, I worked at Hunan University. Hunan University is very

strong in social sciences and humanities. They have rich materials, and strong campus culture. There are all kinds of students' activities during weekends. There are few students' activities at this university, especially on the new campus. It does not influence me much. I can buy very specialized books for my own research, using my grant money. I usually buy books directly. The impact is on students who want to read books.

In the story authored by Zha, an active participant in the university's Student Union, there is an organized protest among liberal arts and social sciences students about the limited channels to obtain materials.

The books we have in the library are very few. We need the internet as an alternative source for research. This semester, we [the Students' Union] did surveys on library usage. In this suburban area, there is a university zone composed of three universities, including this one. All three universities form a library network. Students at our university can check out books from the other two universities, with our universal library card. However, what I do not understand is that, they only provide such services to graduate students. Undergraduate students do not enjoy such services.

Now we [the Students' Union] are negotiating with the library, hoping that we can obtain access to such library services. We have not reached an agreement yet. We learned about students' opinions. They said they had access to very limited resources. ... We [the Students' Union] are their mouthpiece; we feedback their opinions to the management of the library. The library agrees to consider our request.

▶ Chapter 4 University People's Experiences and Perceptions of the Amalgamation and Expansion Polices

The University's admission policy. Against a backdrop of radical university expansion—5 times increase in undergraduate enrolments in 8 years—some humanities and social sciences disciplines are shrinking and facing serious retention problems. Several faculty members from the Law School and the English Department, tell their stories about the university's admission policy that structurally prevents eligible art-bound high-school graduates from entering the university of focus.

High school graduates' university entrance is determined by their scores in one high-stakes test, the Entrance Examination. The high school graduates are divided into two cohorts, science- and art-bound. These two cohorts of students are taking either science or art entrance examination in accordance to their disciplinary choice, and will respectively feed to the natural sciences/technological disciplines, and social sciences/humanities disciplines at the universities. The average scores of science-bound students are usually much higher than that of art-bound students, given the different numbers of subjects tested, and different grading criteria on the tests. After taking appropriate entrance examination, a high-school graduate will fill out a "wish list," listing not only the institutions but also the target departments in the institutions he or she wants to apply for.

Then each university is assigned a threshold admission score (s) by MoE depending on the number of applicants for it. A regular, comprehensive university will be assigned two threshold admission scores, one science score (e. g., 600) and one art score (e. g., 550). The university then works out a hierarchy of admission scores of the individual departments and units on the basis of the threshold score, with the admission scores of the most sought-after and prestigious departments much higher than that of unpopular departments. For instance, the admission score of a university's representatire department, the Department of

Architecture, might be 50 points above the threshold admission score (e. g., 650) and that of the unpopular department, the Department of Astronomy, might be equal to the threshold admission score (e. g., 600). Similarly, a hierarchy exists among admission scores to social sciences/humanities disciplines, with the Department of Economics in the lead and the Department of History at the bottom. Then applicants are admitted to a university, with science-bound students admitted to the natural sciences/technological departments and art-bound students to the social sciences/humanities departments. That is, science- and art-bound students are admitted through two separated channels.

The university of focus, however, as a traditional technological institution, is assigned only one admission score—the science admission score. This means that, although science students are admitted through the normal procedure, the art students have to have exceptionally high scores among the art cohort in order to meet the threshold entrance criterion which is identical to that for science students. In this way, a very small number of art-bound students can be admitted to the humanities and social sciences departments at the university of focus. In order to fill up the vacancies in social sciences and liberal arts departments, the university's Admission Office randomly allocates those science-bound students who are admitted to the university but do not meet the criteria of their target prestigious departments, to humanities and social sciences departments. For instance, a student might be randomly assigned to the Department of Politics and Administration, if his or her score is beyond the university's threshold admission score but below the admission score of the Department of Architecture. As those students are arbitrarily assigned to humanities and social sciences departments in which they do not have desire to stay, retention becomes an utmost challenge for these units. Professor Lu highlights the retention problem in the Law School.

Chapter 4 University People's Experiences and Perceptions of the Amalgamation and Expansion Polices

So every year, we faculty members have a very encumbering task. That is, to convince the new students that legal studies are a good discipline. We try to make them interested. Most of them are thinking about switching to the Architecture and Physics Departments. We have to use every means necessary, such as inviting alumni over to deliver speeches. We hope that the success stories of alumni will convince our new students that legal studies offer them promising careers. However, we inevitably see many of our students switch to other majors in the sophomore year. We cannot help it. It is not that we are a bad department, or that our teaching and academic services disappoint them. It is only because those students are in a wrong place. They did not wish to come to study in our school in the first place. Those who did want to study in our school never had a chance to enter the university; and we are trying to retain students who did not want to stay here. Last year, we only have 18 new students, compared to over 300 in a technological department. And some out of the 18 will be switching majors. This is our situation. Our Dean has talked about separating admission score (s) for art and science students. But it is never enforced. The leaders of our university are technological majors themselves. We have to beg them to pay more attention to social sciences, but they never do.

Professor Zhou, in the Department of English, concurs with professor Lu, and tells a story that her department is not able to set up its own standards of admitting students, but passively accepts the allocated students from the university's Admission Office:

Most of our students are science-bound students.

The students of our department, are assigned to us, from the same pool of students as technological departments.... Our students were never interviewed before they entered this program. All English departments in our country, even though they are located in very small institutions, will interview their students before admitting them. They will select students whose oral English are good. However, among the 50 students we admit each year, there are one third of them whose oral English are not up to standard. It is very difficult for them to study English as a major. They would have been denied if we had the chance to interview them. But we have to admit these students, as they are not interviewed. The university does not allow us to have our own admission standards... The leaders just want us to take in students who are denied by technological and natural sciences departments.

To summarize, the analysis of the interviews with the participants reveals that the expansion policy is, to some extent, viewed positively by participants. For instance, Professor Cao and some others emphasize the widening access, as the universities are more inclusive, with more mixed and diverse student body. But there are multiple contending and competing story lines vis-à-vis the official encoding of the expansion policy. This suggests that instead of being digested for public consciousness, and "distributed and consumed 'harmoniously' as 'common sense' accounts" (Boje, 2001, p.79; see also Chiper, 2006), the expansion policy invites a level of power struggle and resistance, among all of which two salient themes emerge: quality and social equity.

The aggressive undergraduate enrolment expansion between 1999 and 2006 at the university of focus had occurred on top of an infrastructure that had already stretched thin in accommodating its student body. The "quality" of teaching and learning becomes the utmost concern of those on whom quality has direct impact. Students like Wang Li, and Zhang raises the questions about large classes in which lecturing and rote memory are the norm, limited library resources, the lack of faculty- or staff-student interactions; faculty members are concerned with inadequate professional expertise or lowered standards.

Although strong quality assurance mechanisms of teaching and learning are adopted at the national and institutional levels (e. g., the once-five-year national teaching evaluation, the university Dudao Team) (refer to my elaborations in Chapter 5), these approaches from the "top" do not adequately represent quality definitions from the "below"—the students and frontline faculty members. For instance, Wang is expecting his courses in economics theories to be smaller and inquiry-based, with the instructor playing a facilitator role in constructive conversations. Zheng, specializing in Chinese philosophy, is expecting to realize the idealized mentor-student relationship with more "humanitarian care" in the university setting. Likewise, faculty members are reasserting the criteria and standards of their own "guilds" in the interviews. However, the idea on customer satisfaction and professional autonomy is less ingrained in Chinese universities as in their Western counterparts (Gumport, 2000; Morley, 2002), and is further encroached upon in the aggressive expansion process. Wu, a student in the Department of Radio Engineering, critically emphasizes that students' course evaluations are subtly manipulated in order not to exasperate the already intense employer-employee relationship. Professional standards are lowered or not enforceable, according to Wei and Xu, under the post-expansion condition full of job insecurity. Despite preventive and remedial policies, the lowering of standards of university is inevitable in undergraduate expansion, in that it further limits the articulation of quality standards from the "right" channel—from those whose life are directly impacted by the expansion.

The other reoccurring theme in the interviews with university people concerns social equity. Although overall, participants agree about the widening access of university education, there are questions about which sector of the population benefits more from it. An integral part of expansion policy is students' cost sharing, as part of the anticipated revenues of expansion come from increased students' tuitions (Tang & Zuo, 1999; Research Team at Beijing University, 2001; W. L. Li, 2002; J. F. Li & P. Guo, 2004). Sample stories grounded in the personal experiences of Professor Cao, who has close mentoring relationship with students, and Yun, a student from an economically underdeveloped area of China, Northern Jiangsu, indicate that opportunities of college education are more open to the high- but not low-social economic status (SES) students. The expansion policy in China, as elsewhere in the world (McCowan, 207; Yogev, 2007), is accused of accelerating and deepening social stratification.

Among all these, humanities and social sciences disciplines are more vulnerable to the vagaries of the expansion policy, as these disciplines are less well positioned in the national policy discourses on economic development and international integration, and in the university's traditions, to compete for resources and support. Furthermore, due to the fallacy and pitfalls in the university admission policy, some humanities and social sciences disciplines are facing serious retention and survival problems.

Summary

In Chapter 4, I examine university people's experiences with and perceptions of two national HE reform policies, amalgamation and expansion. The analysis of interviews with participants suggest that there are high levels of reconstitution of and resistance towards

▶ Chapter 4 University People's Experiences and Perceptions of the Amalgamation and Expansion Polices

distant national policies in the "situated practices" of administrators, faculty members and students at the university of focus. The results converge to Trowler's (2001) comments that "policy discourse can be understood as polysemic 'text' amenable to alternative readings at variance with that encoded by policy-makers" (p. 184) and Gabriel's (1995) research findings that at an organization, "the workers are not merely submissive to managements' cultural assaults, but dodge, subvert, evade and resist them by creating their sub-cultures and counter-cultures" (p. 478). He further concludes that there is always an unmanaged terrain, a terrain which "is not and cannot be managed, in which people, both individually and in groups, can engage in all kinds of unsupervised, spontaneous activities" (p. 478). The analysis of interviews suggests that national HE reform policies are "blunt instruments" in enabling university change.

Chapter 5
University People's Experiences and Perceptions of Quality Assurance Mechanisms

In this case-study research, in addition to examining the "situated practices" of the amalgamation and expansion policies, I elaborate on the university people's experiences and perceptions of teaching and research quality assurance mechanisms. In Chapter 2, the Literature Review section, I have stated that I want to follow the trajectory of policy dynamics from the international, through the national and to the institutional level, and examine the "situated" policy receptions and reconstructions at the university of focus. In that Chapter, I have elaborated on the rise of audit culture and the "deprofessionalization" of academic professions in the international arena. This background literature provides a macro-context that illuminates what is going on at the national and institutional levels in China. Furthermore, I have explained the major national quality assurance mechanisms in teaching and research in China, and argued that these mechanisms bear with them hidden agenda, which shape universities in a direction that is coherent and consistent with national economic and political interest.

In this Chapter, I intend to present the findings that emerge from my anlaysis of the interviews with faculty members, administrators and students at the university of focus. The national quality assurance mechanisms have direct and indirect impacts on

► Chapter 5 University People's Experiences and Perceptions of Quality Assurance Mechanisms

universities. They not only serve as a framework which university people's behaviors must structure around and adapt to (Brennan & Shah, 2000a; Shore & Wright, 1999, 2000; Trow, 1996a), but also infiltrate and co-opt some normal, day-to-day functions of the university, turning them into a stretched arm of bureaucratic surveillance and regulation of university activities. I present in this chapter, Chapter 5, the two layers of impacts of national quality assurance mechanisms. Furthermore, from the analysis emerges the theme that, instead of mutely accepting the quality assurance mechanisms as given, university people are actively engaging in discursive "displacement, resistance, reconstruction and negotiation" (Trowler, 2001, p. 196). They not only critically reflect on their experiences with the national quality assurance mechanisms, but also mobilize various social resources to cope with them and mitigate the negative impacts to a large extent.

This chapter, the Chapter 5, is divided into three parts.

First, I present university people's experiences with and perceptions of the two rounds of national undergraduate teaching evaluation: a rehearsal in November 2007 and the real evaluation in April 2008. This is the direct impact of the national quality assurance mechanism.

Second, I present how the university's *Dudao* Team is co-opted, serving as an internal teaching assessment mechanism answering to the national undergraduate teaching evaluation with a purpose of standardizing teaching process, and what university people's perceptions and responses are.

Third, I present that the promotion criteria at the university of focus are finding sources in national quality assurance mechanisms. The way the institution seeks to define and assign values to faculty research work—the emphasis on governmental grants, governmental research contest awards, and international journal publications—converges with the elements emphasized in "performance indicators" that national quality bodies set for institutions. National quality assessments typically embody economic and political agenda, and ensure compliance through either awarding or taking away status and resources (Brennan & Shah, 2000a, 2000b; Shore & Wright, 1999 & 2000; Trow, 1996a). The convergence between institutional and national measurements of research performance implies that national quality discourse filters all the way down to institutions and there is a lack of control and ownership of the standards and criteria over their own "guilds" among frontline faculty members at the university of focus. Such phenomena are termed political and bureaucratic authorities overriding the moral authority of professionals (Brennan & Shah, 2000a, 2000b; Finch, 1997) or as the normative dimension replacing the idiosyncratic dimension in faculty assessment (Lincoln, 1983).

Furthermore, I present the evidence that, instead of accepting promotion criteria as given conditions, the frontline faculty members in this case study are highly reflexive and pragmatic, making an active effort in reconstituting and refashioning externally derived languages on research excellence into locally relevant and appropriate terms. Either the faculty members in this sample of interview participants are critically reflexive of the agenda in the external criteria on faculty performance, and adopt "outward conformity" in making efforts for career advancement through formal channels, or they pursue alternative practices that fall out of the contour of the formal evaluative system, but are meaningful and positively sustain the construction of personal, collegiate and professional identities.

Experiences with and Perceptions of the National Undergraduate Teaching Evaluation

By the time I was visiting the university of focus, the memories about the two rounds of National Undergraduate Teaching Evaluation

Chapter 5   University People's Experiences and Perceptions of Quality Assurance Mechanisms

were fresh and vivid in university people's mind: the rehearsal of the evaluation in November, 2007 and the real evaluation in April, 2008. During the rehearsal, faculty members and administrators were engaged in an enormous amount of document preparation work. Then a group of "experts" invited by the leaders of the university of focus inspected the campus, simulating the process of the real evaluation. The "experts" randomly reviewed the documents that included undergraduate students' test papers, graduation theses, experimental reports, held conferences with faculty members and students, and randomly observed classes and labs. The rationale for simulating the evaluation in November, 2007, was to identify and make up as many shortcomings as possible before the visits of the real assessors. The process of the real evaluation in April, 2008 was the same with the rehearsal, albeit that the group of "experts" were invited and appointed by MoE and they rated the university of focus on a few indices which were reported to MoE.

In my interviews with the participants, I asked them to recollect their experiences with the two rounds of the evaluation and comment on those experiences. Faculty members are articulating virulent criticisms on the evaluation which to them is "formalistic through and through" and "making faculty members feel insecure". Undergraduate students, to a large extent, recall the experiences of being instructed to "put their best foot forward" and not to talk carelessly, in order to cope with the two rounds of evaluation. Some of them comment that their educational experiences are mitigated, instead of being improved or enriched by the evaluation. Furthermore, it emerges from the data that the evaluation process intensifies conflicts between existing social groups, and to some extent, empowers administrators and senior faculty members in that they are regarded as safeguards and interpreters of the quality standards. Across most interviews, university people aired the belief that the evaluation is not effective, and the university bounce back to its normal state of being as soon as the external pressures were taken away.

Faculty members' experiences and perceptions of the undergraduate teaching evaluation

Most faculty members and administrators describe the assiduous work devoted to document preparation. Professor Qing, for instance, engages in reviewing students' tests papers in the past few years, adding up the section scores in each test paper and making sure that there is not a single mistake in calculation. Professor Zhu goes over the defense forms of the undergraduate theses she has supervised in the past few years and rewrites the advisor's comments on those theses. Her goal is to fill up the space provided in each form, so that her comments do not appear to be "too concise" or "too hasty" in the eyes of the external assessors. Sheng, a first-year doctoral student, is a teaching assistant to his advisor. As the advisor's former teaching assistants supervised undergraduate students experiments, Sheng's task during the document preparation is to scrutinize all undergraduate students' experiment reports, and fill up the blank spaces, for instance, the time of experiments. For most of the time, he believes that he has to be creative and improvise the information that he has no access to, as those former teaching assistants have graduated and left the university. All faculty members with teaching tasks are engaged in such "putting up cosmetics" work of some sort or another and they are required to arrive on campus before 8:00 a.m. each of the three days when the rehearsal is conducted. In case that their documentation is questioned by the external assessors, they are required to respond immediately and correct that mistake.

Two dramatic instances recounted by faculty members are illustrative of the fact that, the requirement on documentation is

▶ Chapter 5 University People's Experiences and Perceptions of Quality Assurance Mechanisms

exacting and attentive to minute details. The first instance is told by Professor Shi in the Department of Mathematics. As he teaches large lectures in mathematics, at the end of each semester, he enters around 300 students' scores into a single score sheet. Once he recorded a student's score in a wrong line. He corrected the mistake and signed his name in a space near the correction. This score sheet, during the document preparation for the evaluation rehearsal, is pointed out as "not meeting the standards." He is required to submit a new score sheet without a single correction to the University's Office of Teaching Affairs. He complains that recording students' scores becomes a "mission impossible" for him,

> I was asked to record all students' scores again, without a single mistake. I was not allowed to cross out anything. How could you imagine it? Each semester, my class is as big as 300 students. It is very natural for me to make a mistake in recording students' scores, while it is unnatural if I do not make a single mistake. The mistake is of different nature. I make a mistake in entering a student's score. I do not maliciously give the student a score that he/she does not deserve. This is of different nature. Sometimes, you have to use blue and red colors to separate students who pass or fail the tests. I use the blue pen all the time, and do not switch to red color when a score below 60 suddenly appears. I cannot cross out that blue score. I have to start all over again.

The other instance is recalled by Professor Wei. In the final exam of one semester, several of her students got 58 or 59, which were failing scores. Those students who received 59 filed a complaint to the Office of Teaching Affairs. The Office demanded Wei to write a report to justify why she graded these students 58 and 59. In order to save herself from this trouble, she changed the students' grades to 60, allowing them to pass. Now, during this teaching evaluation, all students' test papers are reviewed piece by piece. "The new rule is that teachers should not elevate students' scores for no reason. I am caught for elevating students' grades, for grading students 60 when they only deserved 59, and have to correct such 'miscalculations'."

There are multiple voices in response to the national undergraduate teaching evaluation, among which criticisms dominate.

Professor Lu, who is in charge of the curriculum and instruction in the Law School, views the teaching evaluation in a positive light. As the Law School is nascent and lacks a consensual understanding of how teaching work should be conducted, Professor Lu thinks that the School benefits more from the evaluation than older departments and units which have deeply-entrenched conventions. She states that

> The MoE rates each institution on a few indices. The real purpose is not to fail any institution, but is, through the process of preparation and responding to the "experts," to learn the standard means of doing work... The Law School is newly established. Our school benefits from the assessment in that we learned the standard procedure during the nascent period of the school. We do not have to wrestle with old habits and conventions. We are required to provide detailed documents and follow strict procedures in undergraduate teaching. This left a deep impression on me...

Other faculty members tend to be more critical towards the national undergraduate teaching evaluation, and make comments that resonate with Shore and Wright (1999, 2000), Morely (2002, 2003) and Newton (2002) in their responses to the national teaching evaluation in the United Kingdom. These authors simultaneously refer to the teaching evaluation as "staged performance", rehearsed and performed for the benefits of outside assessors. The teaching evaluation is co-opting everyone at the universities without an option for noncompliance. In Morely's (2002) words, the teaching evaluation is "a comedy of manners, in which all actors, like characters in a Jane Austin novel, play carefully choreographed roles... All the players are skeptical about the rules of the game, and yet all go ahead with a lucid engagement to appease the forces of prosperity and funding" (p. 127). Most faculty members in this sample of interview participants refer to the national teaching evaluation in China as "formalistic", include Professor Lu who tries to see it in a positive light. For instance, Professor Jiang comments that

> The teaching evaluation, in all, is formalistic through and through. We are informed about the evaluation one year in advance. We have time to prepare all the documents according to the guidelines. What the evaluators see are all false, artificial things, while those students who have already graduated will no longer benefit from our assiduous work on their tests and theses.

Professor Zhu concurs with Professor Jiang and asserts that the evaluation is "all about pleasing the external assessors" who do not have contextualized, deep understanding about the teaching and learning practices at the ground level. In some cases, the evaluators are giving conflictual advice, echoing their personal preferences and orientations rather than an empathetic and informed understanding of the sites they are visiting. She gives the example that

> In the first round of evaluation, one expert criticizes that our mission statement is unrealistic and empty. At that time, the mission statement went that we intended to develop ourselves into the first-tier Law School in the

nation. We were advised to set more realistic goals, as our school [formerly a department] is newly established. So we revised our mission statement according to his advice. In a newer version of the mission statement, we humbly stated that the Law School aims to mold law practitioners for the nation. However, in the second round of the evaluation, we were again criticized by the experts. They said that we did not have a long-term, broad goal. We were too myopic, and needed to see tens or even hundreds of years ahead into the future. So we are rather puzzled as how to please the experts. When we had a broad goal, we were criticized as being unrealistic; being practical was seen as near-sighted. Those experts they have different personalities...

Professor Han's comments are, although university people become rather wise to the evaluation after the rehearsal, the fear is there during the real evaluation. She has an acute sense of being monitored and scrutinized, which leads her to comment that the purpose of the evaluation is not to ensure quality, but to make the academics feel insecure, in her words, "to remind us that someone is watching us." She further describes the panic and insecure feelings during the evaluation.

The evaluation is punitive. That means that if you are caught in trouble during the teaching evaluation, you will be laid off. You'll be unemployed ... They are not just threatening us. Each of us feels the pressure, although to a different degree. Of course, the Dean says this because he wants us to do our work well. We have great responsibility... The Dean has made it explicit that... He speaks about this repetitively in the college-wide meetings...

In summary, faculty members at the university of focus provide the details of the preparation work they are obliged to engage in response to the national undergraduate teaching evaluation, which evokes virulent criticisms and strong resistance among them. Despite a few voices affirming the evaluation as an effective mechanism in improving teaching, others are more reflexive and critical, referring to the "formalist" and "artificial" nature of the evaluation. That is, the target of the evaluation is not the genuine, real-life teaching practices but is what is carefully rehearsed and altered to appear good in the eyes of the campus inspectors. Furthermore, some faculty members comment that outside evaluators, in their positions of power, sometimes are making arbitrary comments which reflect the evaluators' personal preferences rather than informed understanding of what is happening at the ground level. Last, the comments about the fear and insecurity faculty members experience resonate with the image of Foucault's Panopticon. The evaluation functions to instill the fear within the faculty members so that they will be policing themselves and acting in accordance to the instilled framework, even when the external pressures are taken away.

Students' experiences with and perceptions of the national undergraduate teaching evaluation

Students' experiences with the national undergraduate teaching evaluation concern being instructed to "put the best foot forward" or talk cleverly. Zha, for instance, emphasizes that she is told to be on time for her 8:00 a.m. class. She says that

> A few days before the experts' visit, our counselor would appear at the gate of the building where the 8:00 a.m. classroom was. She would count the number of students who showed up after 8:00 a.m. After a few days, none of us would be late for the 8:00 a.m. class, as we all got the message.

Bei, a student in the School of Art, says that in a few school-wide meeting mobilizing students to get prepared for the teaching evaluation, it is repeatedly asserted that all students should comment on the university and the School of Art positively, should they be randomly drawn to attend the conferences held by the evaluators, as "careless talk costs money." Rumors go that an evaluator will randomly drop by a classroom, or come up to a student. Bei says that "I know very well how to talk in such situations even if I was not taught to. Negative comments won't help anyone in such situations."

Zhao, an active participant in students' unions and associations, says that all students' organizations receive generous funding in the year of 2007 and 2008, although he suspects that "the good days will not last long". He explains that

> The university will be rated on students' associations and unions. So the university is providing generous funding to us. The evaluators will survey how many students are participating in associations and unions... They will also calculate the percentages of students who participate in such activities... We have more money, and more students are encouraged to join us. If you look around, there are more banners and posters, indicating that the students are holding events and activities, although I do not know what the situations will be like in a year's time. In the years before the evaluation, we did not have sufficient funding. The university leaders are all technological majors. They do not think that students' activities are important. For instance, if we travel outside of the campus, they will be held responsible for the dangers we encounter and they are afraid that some radical students will tarnish the university's image...

▶ Chapter 5   University People's Experiences and Perceptions of Quality Assurance Mechanisms

In addition to reflecting upon their experiences with the national evaluation, students provide the comments that the "standardization" emphasized in the teaching evaluation mitigates against their rich educational experiences. In the evaluation, among many restrictions made on frontline university instructors' classroom practices, one requirement is to attach a "standard" answer sheet to each instructor-made test. Furthermore junior faculty members need to obtain signatures from senior faculty members before the former can distribute the tests to students. Such efforts to "standardize" the instruction not only considerably limit instructors' discretion in their contextualized interactions with students, but also directly impact on students' experiences of education, the "experiential good" (Teixeira et al., 2004). The instructors' immediate coping strategies are to make their tests as simple and the answers as self-evident as possible. According to Sun and Wang, during the two years that the two rounds of evaluation are on, the final term papers are changed to sit-in exams in most of their classes. Sun comments that

> The instructors want to save themselves from the trouble. They gave us sit-in exams with a lot of multiple choices. There are no controversies around the answers to multiple choice questions. Because most associate professors and lecturers are required to attach standard answer sheets to their instructor-made tests for senior professors to review, multiple choice questions at least save their efforts to write up lengthy answers to essay questions. So we go back to memorize text books and answer multiple choices as if we were still high school students.

Empowerment of administrators and senior faculty members in the national teaching evaluation process

Another issue that emerges from the analysis of the interviews with the university participants is that university micro-politics are slightly altered, with administrators empowered in relations to faculty members in general, and senior faculty members acquiring additional power over junior faculty members. The administrator-faculty and senior-junior faculty divide represents the age-old social conflicts on campus (Gornitzka & Larsen, 2004; Massy et al., 1994) and the teaching evaluation serves to further engulf the divide. According to Brennan and Shah (2000a), external quality assessment tends to strengthen the power of institutional management, in that it tends to make decisions and justify the implementation on the basis of the external threat. The interviews in this case study reveal that the national teaching quality assessment targets academics in general, which positions the administrators in roles as interpreters of quality standards and safeguards of university reputation.

For instance, Kong, Director of the Office of the Subunit of Teaching Evaluation, in contrast to faculty members, stresses the necessity of document preparation in the evaluation process. He emphasizes that the "collective wisdom and experiences accumulated from years of administrative practices" are belittled in carrying out the institutional mission.

> Administrators have accumulated years of experiences through concrete practices. Such experiences are important in keeping the university running. I will give you an example of why we stress so much the document preparation. You know about Deng Xiaoping, the late leader of China who used to study at a French university. His university kept an intact record of him, after so many years. However, students' records will be lost or destroyed at a Chinese university in a few years... We want to improve, but we cannot improve without the cooperation and consent from the faculty members. They

say that we are making strict rules, but we are only trying to provide better service to students.

Chu, Vice Secretary General in the School of Economics and Management, and Zhang, staff in the President's Office, both participated in the preparation work for the National Teaching Evaluation in April, 2008. Both recommend more rigorous accountability measures on faculty work, in the name of better serving the student clients. Chu's comments are

> These days, most faculty members have dual tasks and responsibility. Some of them are travelling long distance to carry out personal projects or teaching tasks off the campus. This limits the time and energy they can spend on this campus, where they are employed full time. In face of the national teaching evaluation, some of them are caught in a tremendous amount of preparation work. This is telling, in a certain way, that they are not devoting enough time in teaching before the evaluation. If they did spend enough time before, they do not have to spend time making their work up now. I participated in the mock inspection of student's theses and test papers in our School. Some faculty members are not doing a good job. For instance, you can tell that they wrote very brief responses to students' theses. Students had spent tremendous amount of time and energy writing their undergraduate theses, while faculty members were not giving them constructive feedbacks. So there is reason that the national teaching evaluation has made rules on the length of faculty members' comments on students' theses—such accountability measures should be more rigorously pursued in order that the quality of our university can be improved and the students are better

served...

These statements suggest that, the teaching evaluation process casts the university's management in the interpreter and safeguard roles of the quality standards. This, to some degree, intensifies the lack of "service culture" at Chinese universities. Gornitzka and Larsen (2004) define a "service culture" among U. S. administrators in that they

> See themselves as serving academic staffs, and in doing so they perceive themselves as reactive rather than active. Respect for academic supremacy in governance, and for academic values ... They see themselves as representing a "complementary competence," that they are not competing with academics for areas of competences and responsibility. (pp. 464 – 465)

Ample literature suggests that there are more intense administrator-faculty competitions and conflicts at Chinese universities, with the former playing a more dominant role in determining the day-to-day university affairs (X. M. Xiong, 2005; C. F. Yin & Xia, 2003). The teaching evaluation process, to some degree, accords the "management" in a more powerful position and further alienates the idea of "service culture."

In addition to the administrator-faculty conflict, junior faculty members' discretion over classroom instructions are further constrained and intruded given that they are obliged to obtain endorsement from senior faculty members in accomplishing simple tasks such as making tests and changing students' grades. To standardize teaching, the teaching evaluation process tries to impose standard formulas on contextualized and situated interactions with students, and requires such interactions to be externalized for the sake of outside assessors. So junior faculty members are constantly required to justify every action they take in the classrooms, such as attaching lengthy "standard" answer sheets to the instructor-made tests, and attaching explanations if they want to change students' grades. They need to obtain endorsements and sanctions from senior faculty members before these actions can be completed. Senior faculty members, regarded as the higher-level of technocrat experts, are entrusted into the roles as monitors of junior faculty members to ensure that the standardization is going on in the classrooms. All these reinforce junior faculty members' dependent and subordinate status in relation to senior faculty members. In short, the teaching evaluation process tends to reinforce the existing power structure on campus, according more trust and power to administrators and senior faculty members, while further restricts the professional autonomy and discretion of junior faculty members over their work.

The Uinversity's Dudao Team and Faculty Coping Strategies

I argue that apart from directly impacting on the university people, the national level teaching quality assurance mechanisms at the national level tend to co-opt some of the university's normal functions, turning them into stretched arms in monitoring and supervising the university's quality and day-to-day activities. In the second part of this chapter, Chapter 5, I first examine the mechanism of the University's *Dudao* Team, which, although firmly grounded in the university's tradition, has been co-opted, serving as an internal assessment mechanism answering to the national undergraduate teaching evaluation with a purpose of standardizing teaching process. Second, I illustrate faculty members coping strategies in face of the *Dudao* Team.

As early as 1989, the university's Office of Teaching and Research started to invite senior and retired professors to form a *Dudao* Team, to randomly observe, evaluate and advise on junior faculty members' classes. In 1993, the university started to sponsor annual teaching contests among voluntary participating junior faculty members, with the same team members serving as judges at the contests. Such mechanism sprung out of the necessity of ensuring teaching quality in the drastic rebuilding and expansion of the universities after 1978. As at that time, a great number of fresh-out-of-school undergraduates were recruited to staff the culture-revolution devastated universities, senior professors were invited to mentor and monitor junior faculty members to ensure the continuity of teaching quality.

Although at the beginning, the work of the *Dudao* Team oriented towards "helping" junior faculty members, and participation was voluntary and non-punitive, since 2006, the university has incorporated the annual teaching contests into formal faculty evaluation: holding a third (or better) place in the teaching contests became a teaching criterion for promotion from the lecturer to associate-professor rank. The purpose, according to Kong, a high-ranked administrator, is to better ensure the teaching quality in accordance to the MoE documents. This indicates that the national efforts of "standardizing teaching" have somehow penetrated the mundane and routine practices at the university. Furthermore, each year, the contests only allow 60% of the contestants to pass; the other 40% are forced to reenter the contests in the following year. Thus, for junior faculty members, participation is compulsory and has punitive consequences.

The university's Dudao Team

The mechanism is centralized in that a single university-level team is in charge of the observation and evaluation of all contestants. Although team members are dispersed in most disciplines at the university of focus, the disciplinary disparities are not well respected. For instance, although a member from the English Department is represented in the university-level team, in

▶ Chapter 5 University People's Experiences and Perceptions of Quality Assurance Mechanisms

2006, a lecturer in English was observed and evaluated by three team members, including other two members from the areas of engineering and social sciences. The rationale for building one *Dudao* Team at the university-level, but not multiple teams based on different disciplines, is to prevent nepotism and *guanxi* from influencing and corrupting the function of *Dudao* Team. Professor Xie (team leader) explains that

> ...everyone in a college knows everyone else. For instance, I have worked in the department of mechanical engineering for such a long time. I may not know some junior faculty members, but I know their advisors. The advisors may say to me "the class you are observing is taught by one of my former doctoral students. Is he/she good?" So when I am observing this class, taught by the junior faculty member whose advisor is my friend, I might be constrained by the fact that I know him or her in some way. So we are trying to find a most impartial and objective way to judge the young faculty members. We do not let the social relations influence us.

The judgment of teaching quality is based on the "executive" (or what Friere terms as "banking system") model of teaching and learning (Fenstermacher & Soltis, 2004) in that the emphases are placed on teachers' mastery of the subject matters, delivery techniques, management of time, or even clarity in speech. Students are portrayed as passive receptors, in need of being "absorbed" and encouraged to give feedbacks. For instance, one suggested criterion for a first place winner, according to one team member, is that "95% students are listening attentively." In other words, the teaching contests have a disciplinary and socializing, rather than a generative or innovative effect. Faculty members whose practices fall out of the university's definition of standardized teaching tend to be marginalized. For instance, faculty members with international experiences (e. g., Professor Xu and Professor Yang) comment that "student-centered" elements may be misjudged or not duly recognized. One *Dudao* Team member (Professor Su) talks about his dilemma in evaluating one "bilingual" social sciences class. In the class, students are apparently more interested in learning the equivalent English terms of social sciences theory than the theories themselves. Professor Su says that

> It seems to me that this is a Chinese-English translation rather than a social sciences theory class. The instructor did not get to the content...but there is a high level of involvement of the students...

Furthermore, the local mechanism of teaching quality assurance disproportionally represents "experts'" but not students' views. Although both experts' and students' evaluations count in determining the outcome of the teaching contests, students' course evaluations are not compulsory. The university requires students to fill out course evaluations online only if they want to check their grades of those courses. In my interviews with many students, they do not regularly check grades, especially those "common courses" (like English and Marxism) that they think they have very little chance to fail. Advanced-level students have even less concern for grades than lower-level students. In actuality, experts' rating of teaching performance far outweighs students' perspectives in determining the outcomes of teaching contests.

Faculty members' coping strategies

Although junior faculty members complain that they are "co-opted" without a chance to escape, they simultaneously express a resilient view that the restrictions imposed by the local teaching contests are a temporary phenomenon, as Professor Jiang says that

Chapter 5 University People's Experiences and Perceptions of Quality Assurance Mechanisms

You prepare for a few lessons and try to pass the teaching contest; and you can be on your own again. The tip is that you need to be aware of what experts are expecting or what you should do during the contest. It does not mean that you have to teach this way all your life.

In other words, junior faculty members are practicing "outward conformity" to the university monitoring mechanism on teaching; they relapse into their old teaching practices as soon as the external sanction is away. The lament of Professor Kong, director of the Subunit of Teaching Evaluation, is that "it is impossible to crystallize the standardized teaching" as "you cannot observe them for a life time."

Furthermore, it is a common practice among junior faculty members to reach team members through various *guanxi*, and "move them by a personal story" (Professor Xu). Junior faculty members like Professors Han, Zhu and Zou all talk about the experiences of trying to talk to a *Dudao* Team member they know or they can reach for. Professor Zou says that she told one senior *Dudao* member in her department about her spending 7 years pursuing a doctoral degree in sociology in Hong Kong, meantime all her colleagues moved ahead of her in academic rank. "I have remained in the lecturer's position for over 10 years. It makes quite an emotional impact on people hearing my story," says she. These junior faculty members' strategies suggest that *guanxi* has somehow penetrated the centralized, impartial function of the *Dudao* Team, and plays a role in the outcomes of teaching contests.

Although being a *Dudao* member, Professor Su rejects being perceived as "a stretched arm of the university administration, used to monitor junior faculty members' teaching." His rationale for participating in the team is that "the junior faculty members in my department need to be protected." As the College of Humanities is a relatively minor unit and has very limited representations on the Team, Professor Su reasons that

> More humanities senior faculty member should occupy places in the *Dudao* Team. Or the young faculty members in my department are subject to the arbitrary judgments of the professors who do not understand the realities of teaching a common course [Marxism] in China. Students are resistant towards this course, regardless of the instructors. Our faculty members should not fall victims to this fact, when judged by someone who is not aware of this reality.

Another junior faculty member, Professor Yang's comment is that, feedback from "experts" does not help her as much as that from students. She says that

> Teaching is highly personalized and individualized. Whether *Dudao* members rate me high or low, it has nothing to do with my teaching "effectiveness." My habit is to talk to a few students informally during the middle of a semester. If I am not able to talk to all of them, I pick a few student representatives. I do this semester after semester, because the students are not the same each time.

Yang further explains that as Chinese students are used to the "professor as sage" mode of teaching, she tries to "train" them to think more critically through articulating personal and dissonant opinions. It is not easy, as when she first asks a question, there is sheer and embarrassing silence in the classroom. She tends to hold onto the silence until a student volunteers an answer. She explains that "of course, I will not use this strategy when a *Dudao* observer is in the classroom. Given the waiting time, I will be viewed as a very ineffective instructor in their eyes."

In short, coping strategies proliferate among junior faculty members in face of the university's teaching contests, which, as part of faculty evaluative system for promotion, has been co-opted into the national quality assurance mechanism. Using outward conformity and *guanxi* is the most common practices. For some professors, although being part of the evaluative system, they attribute vastly different meanings to their roles and functions from the official definitions. Furthermore, teaching to some faculty members is informed by their context-specific interactions with students, rather than by the mega-institutional standards. All these suggest that the university's efforts to instill "standardized teaching" through promotion policies are strongly resisted from the below by frontline faculty members.

Research Promotion Criteria and Faculty Coping Strategies

I have argued in Chapter 2, the Literature Review section that, the number of official grants, governmental research contest awards, and international journal publications is the "performance indictors" of the national evaluation of research quality, and explained the hidden international integration and nation-building agenda these "performance indictors" bore. In the third part of Chapter 5, I will continue to argue that the way the institution seeks to define and assign values to faculty work converges with the elements emphasized in the "performance indicators" that national quality bodies set for institutions. Such convergence suggests that, to some extent, the national quality discourses have filtered all the way down to an institution, and co-opted the way the institution chooses to evaluate and reward faculty members work, that is, the way faculty members are promoted. Consequently, there is a lack of ownership and control of the standards and criteria over their own "guilds" among frontline faculty members at the university.

In this third part of Chapter 5, I first describe inductively, in detail, the local criteria of promotion from the lecturer, through associate- to full-professor rank, and of promotion to a doctoral advisor's status. My effort concentrates on illustrating that these criteria are derived from and inherit the hidden agenda in national quality discourses. Then I display a wide array of faculty reflections on and descriptions of their behaviors vis-à-vis the promotion criteria, which suggests that there is a high-level of "political reflexivity" and resistance among frontline faculty members.

Before embarking on these tasks, I prepare the audience familiar with the U.S. promotion and tenure system with some basic facts and background information by explaining the concept of different academic ranks and titles at Chinese universities. Unlike in the United States, most Chinese universities do not have tenure system. There are basically three academic ranks: lecturer, associate professor and full professor. An academic in a lower rank can apply for and be promoted to the next higher rank if he or she both meets the specified institutional criteria and passes the reviews of departmental and university-level academic committees. In the United States, there is a time-frame for obtaining tenure; at Chinese universities, individuals who fail to get promoted can apply again in the future years and can potentially remain at the current level until retirement. In China, doctoral advisor status will only be granted to associate and full professors with institutionally-specified quality—it signifies a high-level of achievements—whereas in the United States, doctoral advisor status is assumed upon employment in most cases.

Research promotion criteria

The research promotion criteria are similar to N. M. Zhang and Y. M. Zhou's (2007) analysis of promotion criteria across different institutions: great stresses are laid on governmental grants, official research contest awards, and international journal publications. This converges with the national framework of research quality assessments. Governmental grant ("vertical" grant) experiences are necessary conditions for all promotions. In order to be promoted to a higher level of academic rank, a lecturer must have been the principal investigator of at least one municipal-level grant, or been one of the first four investigators of at least one provincial or national grant. An associate professor is required to both have been the principle investigator of and be currently conducting at least one provincial or national grant or grant(s) from National Science or Social Science Foundation. The same applies to applicants of doctoral advisor status.

Governmental research contest awards are privileged in faculty evaluation system in that they serve as replacements of other requirements. For instance, a lecturer winning a third or better prize in a provincial or national research contest can be exempted from the grant requirement; winning a second or better prize will have many other barriers—such as years of service and number of publications—lifted for him or her. For an applicant of full-professor rank, winning a first place in provincial teaching contests or a second or better place in provincial or national technological advancement contests will have the requirement on years of service exempted; winning a second or better prize in national teaching, or natural science, invention or technological advancement contests will have all other barriers lifted so that the applicant can be promoted "under special condition."

The requirements on journal and book publications for promotion are complicated and defy easy characterization, given the disparities across different disciplines and the complexity of types of publications. What is consistent across all promotion criteria is the high viability of publications in international or national top-tier journals. An applicant of doctoral advisor status, who has "published in *Science*, *Nature* and other internationally renowned journals within the recent five years can be exempt from all other publication requirements." For an applicant of full-professor rank in humanities and social sciences, one must have published 15 articles in CSSCI journals and one book; however, for those who have at least one publication in *Chinese Social Science*, or two publications in SSCI or A&HCI journals, other journal publication requirement is reduced to as few as five. An applicant of full-professor rank in natural sciences and technologies must have a minimum of five publications, among which two or more should be in SCI journals; an applicant who has published, as the first author, one or more articles in *Science* or *Nature* or other international journals "with an impact factor larger than 15" can be exempted from all other requirements. The same high viability of international-journal publications is evident in the promotion from the lecturer to associate professor rank.

In short, a cursory analysis of the promotion criteria at the university of focus—the emphases on "vertical" funding, and the validation of faculty research through governmental research contests and international journal publications—reflects that promotion criteria are consistent with and co-opted into national measures of research excellence; there is a centralized governmental agenda in validation of faculty work. Pan (2007) comments that "appointment and promotion policies can be used as subtle mechanisms of control without overtly restricting university autonomy and academic freedom, as those who hold power outside the education system may be tempted to influence the appointment and promotion of professors in order to prevent the dispersal of critical thinking that might not be in their interests" (p. 122). Very similar to Ordorika's (2003) description of the mechanism of distributing power and resources under apparent autonomy at a Mexican university, the covert mechanism of faculty promotion in this case is the centripetal force, the "reductionist and simplistic" prescription of teaching and research excellence that aligns with governmental ideological and economic priorities.

Faculty members' coping strategies

Faculty members' experiences with and perceptions of governmental grants. The interview participants are fully aware of the dominant role of "vertical" grants in promotion, as Professor He states that "your private projects ["horizontal" grants] might be referred to, but won't determine anything [in promotion]. It might help you only if you have a competitor whose every other achievement is equal to you." Despite that one administrator is protective of "vertical" grants, others are critical, either of the restrictions "vertical" grants impose on faculty activities or of the hidden agenda these grants bear.

Professor Cao, a high-ranked administrator, tries to rationalize the domination of "vertical" grants, emphasizing that faculty members, the "State-hired" employees, must work for the State, but not grapple with personal rich or serve "private" sponsors. To him, many "horizontal" grants are oriented towards solving lower-end practical problems, which does not contribute to the advanced sciences and technologies of the State. He says that

> In many countries and regions, faculty members are not allowed to apply for "horizontal" funding. The natural responsibility of faculty members, in addition to teaching, is to undertake the research projects of the State. Also, Tokyo University in Japan is like this... I don't think "horizontal" funding should be counted [in promotion] ... In this particular stage of [economic] development, China is not highly industrialized. The faculty members are owners of the most advanced science and technological knowledge. It does not need much technology to solve the

problems the private companies face. "Horizontal" funding does not elevate faculty members' ability, but only brings good money to them. Many faculty members are getting rich, but they are not pushed towards higher achievements...

Others are quite critical of the fact that conducting "vertical" grants constitutes a necessary condition for promotion. "Vertical" funding is extremely meager and limited in scope. The competition for an extremely limited pool of grants constrains faculty members' chances of being promoted. Professor Qing talks about his experience of applying for a grant from the National Science Foundation.

... there are around 100 grants in the area of mathematics. The chances to get the grants are very slim, as these grants need to be divided by all universities. It is very difficult for me to be successful in applying. I am referring to my recent grant. I applied in 2004... It is very difficult. I applied three times, successively in three years. The average success rate is 20%. I applied for three years, so the chance for me to be successful is 33%. So I am among the lucky people.

Professor Tao speaks more reflexively and critically about the "vertical" grants in that they carry governmental ideological agenda, "their" definitions of what is important and impending.

But I think that applying for a grant is different from that in the United States. When you are applying, you should not be considering what you want to do, but what the fund providers want you to do. This is related to the big environment. For instance, most of the projects in the year of 2007 were on building a "harmonious society." You must pay attention to this when you are applying.

▶ Chapter 5　University People's Experiences and Perceptions of Quality Assurance Mechanisms

Some faculty members express a conflict of identity and confusion over what constitute "a proper academic" while choosing between "vertical" and "horizontal" grants. Some others attribute multiple alternative meanings to conducting "horizontal" grants so that, although excluded from formal faculty evaluative system, "horizontal" grants sustain the positive construction of professional and collegiate identities, and the day-to-day normal functions of the university.

For junior faculty members like Professor Xu, the official prescription of "vertical" grants "limit the options available for thought and its articulation" (Trowler, 2001). He felt a necessity to be co-opted into the official discourses in order to be a "proper academic," as he says that

> Outside of the university, I am somebody. I am referred to as a "professor" or "expert." But inside the university, as an associate professor that has not been promoted to full professor yet, some people will probably advise me that I need to "prioritize" my tasks. I do not mean that those people are malicious or jealous. I think they are well intentioned...like my former advisor...

Others attribute multiple meanings to "horizontal" grants so that they are indispensible to the normal, day-to-day functions of the university. For those "applied" fields that the validity of research is justified by the relevance to practice, or the research must be sustained by empirical data obtained from practice, engaging in "horizontal" grants might be an inevitable choice. For instance, in the Law School, faculty members are responding to the accusation that they are practicing law at the expenses of teaching and research, as Professor Lu says that

> We find that although practicing law is very time-consuming, it informs teaching in a very positive way.

We faculty members in the Law School have a good reputation for teaching. In the most recent four years, we ranked 4th place or higher in teaching at the university. It is quite a remarkable achievement to rank so high among all the departments and colleges at the university. At our conferences with the students, students told us that they benefited from the cases that were from faculty members' own experiences. All those cases were grounded in reality, and very vivid. So it is good for faculty members to incorporate their practical experiences into teaching. They can develop such experiences into academic articles. It is easier to publish articles with empirical evidence.

The other reason for involving with "horizontal" grants is to develop areas that are "avant garde," not sanctioned by official discourses but are significant to the faculty members' research community. The human rights research, for instance, touts some faculty members' time and energy, although it may not be recognized as worthwhile in the formal evaluation. Professor He is acutely aware that he is as much a member of his scholarly community as he is an employee of the institution. Collaboration with and recognition from (international) peers might be more significant for him.

We set up a center for human rights studies... We have close contact with Northern European countries, Britain and the Ford Foundation. We receive funding from them. Such money is very important to our research on human rights, and collaboration with foreign countries. We have many chances of visiting and communicating with foreign countries. We provide training on human rights law for our faculty members.

▶ Chapter 5 University People's Experiences and Perceptions of Quality Assurance Mechanisms

> The human rights law is a newly emerging discipline in China... It is very helpful to research and teaching.

For the technological and natural sciences faculty members, "horizontal" grants are essential in maintaining the normal functions of their departments and colleges, although excluded from their formal evaluation. Professor Shi regards "horizontal" grants as the "life blood" with which the university operates and survives. Professor Qing explains that although "horizontal" grants are not as prestigious, they are usually large in sizes. In doctoral-student quota allocation—the total number of doctoral students an institution can admit each year is centrally determined by MoE, and then allocated to each doctoral advisor in departments and colleges by the Graduate Admission Office—the number and sizes of a doctoral advisor's "horizontal" grants determine the number of doctoral students a doctoral advisor can admit, as "cultivating students needs money". According to Professor Qi, students prefer faculty members who have good industrial connections, as many of them expect to be introduced to the networks in industries. Ironically, although the official discourses on research excellence exclude "horizontal" grants, administrators in allocating graduate-student quota and students in selecting academic advisors, all attribute central importance to "horizontal grants." "Horizontal" grants serve to maintain some indispensible functions of the university, such as student advising and research.

Faculty members' experiences with and perceptions of official research contest awards. Professor Wei sheds doubt on the validity of official research contest awards as indicators of research quality and achievements. She says that the review process in the contest is biased, with the reviewers serving both as "referees and the players of the sport games they are playing."

When you compare the number of national awards of

a university in Beijing, and that of a university located in other places of China, you will be very surprised about the gap between these two universities. A university in Beijing usually beats its peers by an overwhelming number of research awards. This does not mean that researchers in other places are weaker, it is only because the university in Beijing is located in the center of politics. It is more accessible to personal networks that determine the quality of the research.

Some faculty members use official research contests strategically, as a means to "returning" to the official discourses on excellence, so as to challenge the colonizing fixed ideas on what is important and excellent. The collective experience of the Department of Politics and Administration is that, it is not able to obtain any official funding to publish the book series collaborated by its faculty members. In 2003, the book series were finally sponsored by a local real estate merchant, after repeated "dirty" bargain and compromise, on condition that the private sponsor is listed as one of the editors. The book series were received exceptionally well, with two books winning local and national book contests. When commenting on the significance of award winning, Professor Su, the then head of the department emphasizes that it did not bring him any personal good apart from the symbolic reward money, as he has all in his age. But the awards made some difference, as the university leaders, technological majors themselves, somehow altered their mindset that "humanities research does not need investments." Furthermore, as the topics of these books rose out of grass-root faculty members' own academic engagement, seeing them juxtaposed with officially approved orthodox topics is groundbreaking.

Faculty members' experiences with and perceptions of journal publications. In general, there is a wider acceptance among natural sciences/technologies faculty members of the integration of SCI journal publications into faculty promotion criteria. Exchange, cooperation and circulation of research at international rather than national level is regarded as a scholarly norm among them. In contrast, there are more controversies and disputes among social sciences/humanities faculty members with regard to tying the number of SSCI or A&HCI publications to promotion. To them, the use of social sciences or arts and humanities citation index systems as indicators of research quality is arbitrary and detrimental to indigenous research. Moreover, these faculty members focus their criticisms on CSSCI journals (the Chinese equivalent of SSCI journals), seeing that these journals are too corrupted by administrative control, fee paying, and personal relations to designate the quality of publications in them.

According to Professor Xu in the Department of Radio Engineering, when thinking about submitting a journal, he naturally chooses journals of an international rather than a national scope. He says that "I need to publish my articles in some internationally renowned journals, so that my research can be distributed to and recognized by a larger scope of audience."

Sheng, a doctoral student in the Department of Chemistry, deems the English language as the "tool without which you are virtually blind." As an ethnic minority in Northern China, he learned his ethnic language, Mongol, in the place of English, from his elementary to undergraduate years. After completing his undergraduate studies, he took off years to learn English in order to meet the foreign-language requirement in the graduate programs in most flagship universities. Reflecting on his past experiences, he says that these years are not wasted, given the significant role the English language is playing in his academic life. Now he has co-authored several articles with his advisor, including one that is published in *Science*. He says that

In my area of study, I rely on the literature in English to conduct the study. Those who learn German or Japanese as foreign languages are limited in the literature they can cover. So you cannot be exempted from learning English. My classmates who learned German or Japanese as foreign languages have difficulty in reading the literature in our area. Even if they have conducted the experiments, they can only publish in Chinese. It is not possible for them to write in English and let more people know what they are doing.

In comparison to the academics in the area of natural sciences and technologies, social sciences and humanities faculty members' views towards publishing in SSCI or A&HCI journals are more ambivalent and divided. Furthermore, they see the CSSCI journals, Chinese equivalents to SSCI journals, as corrupted. In other words, using either SSCI or A&HCI or CSSCI as designations of the quality of publications is seen as a violation of their professional judgments of research quality.

Some of the social sciences and humanities faculty members raise the issue of the marginalization of the regional and indigenous studies in the current system of quality designation. R. Yang (2004) comments that, "any knowledge that does not belong to the [Western knowledge] system is not knowledge, simply because it is not circulating internationally" (p. 190). Professor He's criticisms echo Yang that

Our area of research has very obvious regional and political markers. If you want to publish in international journals... They look down upon our special social system ... They think that legal studies in China... Does China have legal studies?

Professor Yang, an overseas returnee (colloquially called *haigui*) emphasizes the "misuse" of journal index systems as designations of research quality. To her, the original purpose of either SCI or SSCI or A&HCI has nothing to do with quality designation; these indices are used as readers' guide, like an anthology. The overemphasis on SSCI or A&HCI publications greatly limits her choices of journals, as only a few journals in her area are included. She says that "while there are hundreds of journals in my area out there, only around ten in my area are arbitrarily included. This greatly limits my choices while I am making a decision on submitting an article."

Given that most social sciences and humanities faculty members are not publishing in English, a Chinese equivalent journal index system, CSSCI, is used in determining the quality of publications in Chinese. Criticisms are directed at CSSCI as being corrupted by fee paying, personal networks, and administrative control. For instance, Professor Jiang says that

> In academia in China, there is strong administrative control ... The journals belong to the governmental administrative units... The higher the administrative rank, the more influence a journal has... The *Chinese Social Science* is the top-tier journal in China, as it affiliates to the Chinese Academy of Social Science.

In all, as Professor Su says, the use of journal index systems as indictors of quality is created for the convenience of the officials in the educational bureaus who are detached from frontline research. They tend to conveniently count the number of publications that appear in journals of "high quality," while not focusing on the contents. This to him is a token of the lack of ownership and control over the standards and criteria of the academics' own profession, and is substantially damaging to Chinese academia. He jokingly spells out SCI as "stupid Chinese idea" and SSCI as "super stupid Chinese idea."

Amalgamation, Expansion, Quality Assurance and Innovations: A Case Study on a Key University in China ◀

Summary

This chapter, the Chapter 5, displays substantial empirical data on university people's perceptions of and responses to national quality assurance mechanisms. The first part of the chapter is on the university people's direct experiences with and perceptions of the two rounds of national undergraduate teaching evaluation in November 2007 and April 2008. The second and third parts of the chapter focuse on how national quality assurance mechanisms co-opt normal functions of the university, such as the *Dudao* team and faculty promotion, and turn the latter into stretched arms of quality monitoring and control. The university people display a high degree of "political reflexivity" and resilience. Instead of mutely accepting these mechanisms as given, they either critically unravel the hidden agendas embedded, or mobilize multiple resources in turning these mechanisms into locally relevant terms and practices.

Chapter 6
Innovative Ideas and Practices at the University of Focus

In Chapter 4 and Chapter 5, I have examined the implementation or "situated practices" of national HE reform policies at the university of focus: the amalgamation, expansion and quality assurance policies. The findings suggest that the national HE reform grand narratives encounter a high level of resistance and reconstitution at the ground level by faculty members, administrators and students. This brings challenges to the traditional models of policymaking and organizational change.

The assumption underlying the traditional model of centralized, "staircase" policymaking is that, as long as each step in the policy genesis is "scientific" and supported by uninterested data, there is no problem that the policy goals can be realized in the implementation, as if the policies were carried out in a social vacuum (deLeon & deLeon, 2002a, 2002b; Kaplan, 1986; Sabatier, 2005; Trowler, 2002). Likewise, in the traditional model of organizational change, change is seen to be enabled by an exogenous agency or agent (person or circumstances) by applying certain forces—political and managerial requests, orders and commands, for instance. When the organization (the object) fails to move, or does not effectively move, it means it resists and ways must be found to overcome the resistance, through applying stronger forces.

Given these deeply-entrenched models of policymaking and

organizational change, the HE reforms in China since the economic liberation in 1978 are most likely to be pursued in a centralized, top-down manner (X. F. Chen, 2006; B. Chen & Yuan, 2000; Gan & L. L. Wan, 2006; Y. C. Lin, 2007; M. Yang, 2006; S. Zhao, 2007). Even in a neoliberal context where decentralization, deregulation, entrepreneurship and local innovations are the norm (see my discussions in Chapter 1), HE reforms in China are characterized as "centralized decentralization" or governmental "steering at distance" (Kalsen, 2000; Mok, 2004; R. Yang et al., 2007; Vidovich, 2002).

In this chapter, the Chapter 6, I examine local innovations in teaching, research, administration, curricula, and all kinds of "unexpected" places at the university of focus (Button, 2003). The "innovations" under investigation range from small-scale changes to individual practices, through new module and formal procedure changes, to large-scale funded projects. I attempt to describe inductively, what innovations are, through the university people's discursive renderings of the innovative incidences from their perspectives. My approach is "grounded," that is, I do not have a preconceived idea on what innovations are, but invite local people to tell their views and opinions on innovative ideas or practices. The meanings of innovations (what they are, what they are not, how do they work out, what are the impediments to innovations, etc.) gradually emerge through local people' comments and telling.

Such comments on innovations are significant, as they are part of the university people's personal meaning systems, in harmony with individuals' perceptions of organizational purposes, and thus the embodiment of genuine changes at the organizational level. Change in educational setting, as Askling and Stensaker (2002) maintain, rarely happens by decree; an inevitable prerequisite to successful change is the negotiated social construction towards consensus building.

▶ Chapter 6　Innovative Ideas and Practices at the University of Focus

　　Through inductively describing the innovative ideas and practices, I am attempting to illustrate an alternative model on organizational change. I have raised questions on the traditional models of policymaking and organizational change in Chapter 4 and Chapter 5, given the high level of resistance and reconstitution of national HE reform policies in the "situated practices" of administrators, faculty members and students. In contrast, changes that grow out internally from the organization, although sometimes small-scale and sporadic, are more solidly grounded in general acceptance and are more likely to accumulate to significant transformations (Clark, 1983; 1998). We often hear stories about centralized governmental reform efforts that are frustrated by "intractable" problems in educational institutions which remain resilient and keep bouncing back to pre-reform conditions (Owens, 1998). We also hear stories about how some local practices prosper and proliferate, despite all the impediments that work against them. Just as Trowler (2002) comments that "policies are always incomplete in so far as they relate to or map on the 'wild profusion' of local practices. Policies are crude and simple. Practice is sophisticated, contingent, complex and unstable" (p. 16). Through describing the "real" and concrete ideas and practices at the local level, one learns about the "real" and concrete ways through which the university of focus changes.

　　In the following parts of Chapter 6, I try to uncover the properties of localized, small-scale, spontaneous innovations as alternative sources of organizational change.

Five Properties of Local Innovations

Innovations are entrepreneurial

　　First, according to the comments made by administrators,

faculty members and students, innovative incidences are "entrepreneurial" (Clark, 1998). The university of focus is increasingly engaging in market or market-like behaviors to generate external resources. Social sciences and humanities disciplines are involved in "adaptive" or "survival" innovations in a context of meager public resources, such as commercialization of instructions and securing private funding. Natural sciences and technologies units are engaged in technological transfer, patenting, etc. Universities, colleges, departments or even individual faculty members investing in or owning businesses is viewed as unusual, if not grotesque in the perspective of Mohrman (2003), an American observer. But it is constantly cited as incidences of innovations at the university of focus.

One particular example of entrepreneurial innovations, cited by Professor Qing, is that economic incentives are used to reinforce outstanding teaching and research work, as in a business corporation where bonus pay is used to recognize a salesperson's volume of sales. According to Professor Qing in the Department of Mathematics, all faculty members at the university of focus are divided into a hierarchy of 13 levels, with the bonus pay in an upper level significantly higher than that in a lower level. All faculty members are reviewed every three years for their teaching performance and scholarly outputs, the results of which will determine their positions in the hierarchy. Lagging behind one's peers in teaching and research achievements means not only lowering of academic rank, but also considerable reduction in bonus pay. This reward and sanction mechanism, Qing explains, is modeled on that in business corporations. Qing says that

> All the faculty members at the university are divided into 13 levels. There are three levels among full professors. The members of the Chinese Science Academia are the natural first-level professors. The

President and the Secretary General of the university are also classified as the first-level professors. There are a small proportion of faculty members that are second-level professors. The rest of the full professors are of the third level ... I was appointed to a second-level position, because at that time I was coaching undergraduate students for an inter-university math competition. The second-level title was directly given to me; I did not have to go through the review process as others. As a second-rank professor, I was offered ￥26,000 bonus pay per year. So the bonus pay system significantly augments what I earn each year. It elevates my living standards to a considerable degree.

Such innovations hardly bear any air of novelty. Rich literature has documented "entrepreneurialism" "academic capitalism" or the "enterprising university" elsewhere; some researchers are more affirmative towards such phenomena (e. g., Cambell & Slaughter, 1999; Clark, 1998; Dearlove, 1998; Slaughter & Rhoades, 2004; Etzkowitz, Webster, Gebhardt & Terra, 2000) and some others are more critical (Trowler, 2001; Marginson & Considine, 2000). The corporate mode of reward (reward on the basis of job performance) as raised by Professor Qing is evident in some Western "core" countries, and some other universities in China.

In some Western "core" countries, for instance, in the United States and Britain, the traditional collegial governance structure and tenure system are attacked on the basis of inefficiency (Barrows, 2001; Boer, 1996; Trolwer, 1998). In both countries, there is evidence that academics are increasingly hired on a part-time basis in order to eliminate "time serving complacency and generate motivation for writing and research" (Morley, 2002, p. 130; see also Slaguthter & Rhoades, 2004; Torrres & Schugurensky, 2002). In some other universities in China, such as Shandong

Agriculture University, Beijing University and Zhongshan University, an academic will be promoted to or demoted from any academic rank depending on teaching and research performance (Tian, 2006).

Using economic incentives to stimulate teaching and research productivity may constitute objects of criticisms elsewhere, for instance, such mechanism may be accused of compromising faculty members' positions in independent social critique. At the university of focus, economic rewards as incentives for teaching and research seem to have wide acceptance.

Innovations are ambiguous

Second, innovations are ambiguous. There are no existing guidelines concerning how these activities should be conducted. Sometimes they fall out of the existing moral framework of judgment, so that controversies arise around them. Waite and Allen (2003) point out that, what are viewed as "resourceful" measures to generate external resources in a Chinese context are sometimes unethical and condemned if judged by Western standards. Even the interview participants themselves are ambivalent, having mixed feelings towards the innovative practices they are commenting on.

In Chapter 5, I have given the example of the Department of Politics and Administration accepting some funding from a private donor, a real estate merchant in Zhejiang to publish the book series collaborated by its faculty members. In return, the private donor is listed as one of the editors in chief of the book series. This same example is cited by Professor Su as an innovative incidence that causes a moral dilemma. On the one hand, the funding from a private real estate merchant brings sustained benefits to the department. The department not only is able to publish the current book series, but also attracts continuous resources after the book series has become a big success. On the other hand, "dirty deals" which comprise Su's professional standing have to be made, in order to secure the initial funding. For instance, he has to agree to list the private donor as one of the editors in chief. "This creates the impression that we intellectuals can be purchased," he says.

Professor Zhu, while telling a story about faculty promotion, encounters similar moral ambivalence in judgment. Two of her colleagues were promoted as university-appointed professors (*xiaoping jiaoshou*) by serving as legal consultants for the university. She is torn between two contradictory ideas that faculty members' contributions to the university need to be recognized, but should not be exchanged for academic titles. She comments that

> Two of my colleagues contribute a lot to the university, by being legal consultants for the university. They saved the university from many economic losses. This is a way they contribute to the university. Later they were turned into university-appointed professors (*xiaopingjiaoshou*). University-appointed professor is a unique academic rank, very specific to the Chinese context which you probably won't be able to find in foreign countries. It means that they can print the title "professor" on their business cards. That is, they can claim themselves to be full professors while outside the university; but within the university, they are still associate professors. Their salaries are still of an associate professor's level and we colleagues who know their backgrounds do not recognize them as full professors.

Zhu continues to explain that university-appointed professors are alternatively termed as "professors with hats" (*daimao jiaoshou*). It means that there are conditions for them to be recognized as full professors, unlike a normal full professor who will be universally recognized. Such title is used by the university as recognitions to those who have contributed to the university in some, although not academically recognizable, ways. Zhu expresses the dilemma in judgment she encounters.

> This is a very great incentive for people to work for the university. My two colleagues are using their expertise to serve the university, although they can choose to be legal consultants elsewhere. However, I think that academic titles should not be abused. All the others are evaluated by the departmental and the university's academic committees by the number and quality of their publications, but these two colleagues ascend to the academic titles in such an easy manner.

The moral ambivalence Zhu encounters echoes the disputes and debates about broadening the concept of scholarship to incorporate public service into faculty members' promotion in some Western "core" countries like the United States and Britain. Fairwheather (1996) and Bridgman (2007) both advocate "making knowledge and technology transfer a central part of the public service role for faculty, and [about] enhancing the value of public service in personnel decisions" (Feairwheather, p. 9). These authors simultaneously recognize the difficulty in integrating public service elements in face of the traditionally research-oriented reward structure (e.g., emphasis on establishing a track of journal publications).

Professor Xu raises the issue of having doctoral students working in companies owned by their professors. Doctoral students may be exploited as underpaid labors while practical experiences may be valuable for them. He says that

> I know some famous doctoral supervisors; they have large-scale companies, as their research results are transferrable to economic productivity. I know some other

famous doctoral supervisors who recruit doctoral students to work for their companies for 2 years. The 2-year work has nothing to do with the graduate students' dissertations. After 2 years, students come back to do theoretical research. We cannot tell if working for the supervisors' companies is good for the students. This detracts the students from their study. But the students receive scholarships. Many students will work part-time elsewhere to support themselves if they are not working in their advisors' companies. But this is not important. The most important thing for the students is that they have the experiences and ability. Many students are competing for such opportunities as they want to network with people in the trade. Knowing people is much more important than getting good grades.

In short, all these innovative incidences university people tell pose moral dilemma. It is difficult to tell whether such practices open up new possibilities, or jeopardize academic values and professional identities. The interview participants themselves are involved in conflictual feelings and therefore withhold judgments.

Innovations need to work against various impediments

Third, innovations need to work against various impediments, sometimes with success and sometimes without. Novel ideas and practices sometimes encounter adverse environment. Sometimes, the existing discourse frames are too overpowering that novel ideas and practices do not have a chance to grow. Sometimes organizational change is path dependent (Trowler, 1998; Krucken, 2003); modification in one element does not fit into the surrounding elements, so that the innovation dies down. In other words, there are no book recipes for innovative practices and ideas; they are context-specific. Actors need to test water step by step, in an ill-defined, uncertain, complex and unstable environment. The "people factor" is attributed to as the utmost impediment in the stabilization and diffusion of innovative practices. Actors (especially those in leadership positions) coming to or leaving the scene will affect the innovative practices in most significant ways.

Professor Lu tells a story about how the Law School restructures its adjunct law firm three times in order to dodge or evade the State's regulations. The Law School turns out to be resilient and pragmatic in coping with various sanctions and impediments that work against it. As early as 1995 when the Department of Law (later expands into the Law School) was first established, it established an adjunct law firm which was named after the university of focus and was staffed by the entire faculty in the department. The law firm handled the university's legal problems as a return for using the university's name. But in 2000, the law firm was prohibited by the new national regulation which forbade law schools to own adjunct law firms. So the Department of Law hired three full-time lawyers from other places and registered the law firm under their names, although the entire faculty were still part-time employees there. After a while, the State's Juridical Department pointed out that the law firm still belonged to the university, which led to a second restructuring. The law firm owned by the Department merged with another law firm, which now no longer uses the university's brand name. The new firm has 30 full-time lawyers, with all the law-school faculty members working as part-time lawyers. As a result, faculty members benefit as individuals by participating in the law firm as part-time lawyers, but the firm has nothing to do with the Law School or university anymore.

Professor Lu further explains that the State's rationale is to protect full-time lawyers.

It is foul competition for them, if we faculty

members, who have secured employment already, at the same time, have a share in the trade which those full-time lawyers rely on for a living. This is one of the reasons, at least according to my understanding, for the law firm affiliated to our School to be restructured several times.

According to Professor Tao, Associate Dean of the College of Humanities, rules, regulations and bylaws are rigid, but are often "negotiable." An innovation for her, to a certain extent, means negotiating the regulations and rules to one's advantage. She tells a story about how to negotiate for larger students' quota for the College's MPA program.

> We hope that we have a larger admission quota, within the range that the State allows. But the university sees the problem from a different angle. For instance, they think that if our admission scores are too low, the university will "lose face. "We think we should maximize admissions, as long as it is allowed by MoE. We have to interact with the Graduate College again and again on this issue. To be more frank, we are bargaining with them. This is the way we interact to solve problems. We interact with the administrators in charge of students' cultivation. If everyone does the work according to the rules and regulations, our work will be greatly limited. So we have to be innovative and resourceful, in negotiating the rules and regulations to our advantage.

Unlike the success cases of the Law School restructuring its adjunct law firm several times, and the MPA program negotiating for more admission quota, there are many cases of nascent innovations that do not grow or last, as the adversities against them are too strong. This in some way confirms the path dependency theory on organizational change (e. g. , Trowler, 1998; Krucken, 2003).

That is, modifications in one element tend to be unsuccessful when all other elements are working against it. Examples of such innovative attempts are many. According to Dou, Vice Director of the university's Office of Public Relations, the university's two Admission Units, Undergraduate Admission Unit in the Office of Students' Affairs and Graduate Admission Unit in the Graduate College, merged in 2003. The merger was motivated by the prospect of efficiency gains through reducing unit redundancy. However, such innovation was ephemeral, lasting only a few months. The two former units were respectively answering to different higher-level units at the university of focus and in the provincial Educational Bureau. This created a difficult situation for the new comprehensive unit to respond to. So the merger was disintegrated in three months' time.

Sometimes, "people factor" turns out to be the determining variable in the success or failure of an innovation. According to Professor Shi, the innovative instructional program in his department terminated because "new leaders in the Graduate College do not like this program." Here is a detailed story.

> We collaborated with an institution in Ningbo. This for-profit instructional program has around 10 years of history. We provided training at Master's level for students in this program. We sent faculty members over to our partner institution in Ningbo, where the training took place. We used the names of our department and our partner institution in order to attract students. The Graduate College consented to this program. The program has lasted nearly 10 years now, because we had a good supply of students. Ningbo is really an economically well-to-do area in China. Its municipal government reimburses its residents for expenditures on education and training, so we have a good supply of students in this program.

He further explains that the program has to be terminated, because the new leaders in the Graduate College did not consent to this program.

> But this year, our program has to come to an end... We cannot use the brand name of our university to attract students, and our partner institution is not prestigious at all, so students are reluctant to enter this program any more, although we send the same faculty members over. We have to terminate this training program, due to low enrolments this year.

He further comments that in China, a lot of things depend on social networking, especially the whims and preferences of the leaders. Leaders coming to or leaving posts will have great impacts on what people are doing.

In short, there are a "wild profusion" of innovative practices in the university setting, despite all the impediments against them. Some innovations are short-lived, due to organizational inertia. Given the high-context culture in China, innovation means negotiating, bargaining and compromising in day to day and face to face interactions.

Innovations and institutionalization are mutually exclusive

Most participants telling stories about innovative practices agree that innovations should not be "institutionalized." That is, when innovative ideas and practices are crystallized into policies and reinforced in a large scale, they lose all the vitality and dynamism and turn into a new source of constraint and burden. Innovations depend heavily on the specific local circumstances, and deep commitments of the local participants; there are no textbook recipes on what innovations should be. Trowler (2001) says that policies are simple and crude while practices are sophisticated, complex and unstable. Regulating practices through policies inevitably creates outliers and exceptions that do not fit into the policy frame. So innovations resist crystallization and "institutionalization." Krucken (2003), in his study of technological transfer at German universities, finds out that when "entrepreneurial science" became a norm in the late 1980s, and transfer offices were established all over German universities to cope with the political pressures, people started to resist such offices as "an expression of bureaucratic power rather than functional units for fostering university-industry ties" (p. 322). The real technological transfer follows a personalized, informal pattern, for instance, the networking between scientists and industrialists seldom goes through the formal structure of the university. Thus the author concludes that the idea on technological transfer offices starts as an innovative project but ends up as an impediment to real transfer when such idea is standardized and reinforced in a large scale.

Likewise, Findlow (2008) describes the fundamental contradiction and paradox in the efforts to "program" innovations in England. As promoting and facilitating innovations has been one of the major goals of the new higher education discourse, universities are provided with large amount of funding to encourage innovations at the ground level. But the funded innovative programs are fundamentally constrained and prohibited by institutional accountability mechanism which requires innovative projects to demonstrate measureable (salable) results, fall into clearly-defined timeline, minimize risks, etc. Thus, Findlow concludes that innovative efforts "pursued through institutional schema" are doomed to fail.

Teams and groups are the basic units of innovative practices

Teams and groups are critical to innovative practices. Clark

(1998) believes that "groups, large and small—central and departmental—of faculty and administrators (and sometimes students) can fashion new structures, processes, and orientations" (p. 5). In a similar manner, Slaughter and Rhoades (2004; see also Slaughter & Lesile, 2001) maintain that teams are the basis for academic capitalism at universities. These authors believe that in a knowledge-intensive organization as a university, professionals (e. g., faculty members and administrators) have relative autonomy and discretion over their work. They are free to form either stable or volatile organizational subunits or coalitions either with members within the same institution, or members from other institutions as private corporations. Slaughter and Lesile state that these subunits or coalitions can "often restructure themselves to take advantage of the mechanism that enable them to engage in market opportunities" (p. 156). So Slaughter and Rhoades conclude that academic capitalist activities are often accomplished by these restructured subunits or "networks" of actors. In short, self-organizing teams are deemed as the locus where changes and innovations occur. It is in teams that people exchange ideas and thoughts so as to "enrich, interweave and expand our understanding of particular issues or phenomena" (Lueddeke, 1999, p. 274). Differences in social status are lessened so that the whole team converges on "shared values, respect, concern and appreciation" (p. 274).

In this study, university people attribute centrality to team collaborations as ways to initiate and realize innovations. Professor Jiang in the Department of Politics and Administration, for instance, describes the doctoral salon as a spontaneous, self-organizing team which provides a shelter from the penetration of administrative influences.

> Despite the fact that administrators are feeling more supreme than us, it is us academics that make the wheel of the university running. I will normally go home and do

my own research after teaching classes. But I will attend the activities of my teaching and research unit, and the discussions in the doctoral salon. The doctoral salon is a spontaneous organization among us academics. It has a history of several years. Academics and students across several disciplines attended the salon each Saturday. As I am in charge of the key to the conference room, I participate each Saturday. I like to interact with my fellow academics, through which new ideas spark. I think it is such small spontaneous unions and organizations that make the university move. Especially, academic traditions are nurtured and carried on. Sometimes, administrative attempts to change university in this and that way only make trouble.

The retired Professor, Xie, speaks in reminiscence about the team culture at the university of focus before the economic liberation in 1978. He criticizes the tendency to separate teaching and research at the university, whereas before 1978, all teaching-only faculty members were incorporated into teaching and research units with other faculty members. They were required to conduct research projects. He feels strongly that such practices should be restored.

The faculty members of common courses must participate in research projects. There is some difficulty for faculty members who teach common courses, such as math, physics, chemistry, and English to engage in research. They have heavy work load, and great burden, and difficulty in finding time for research. But it is necessary for them to participate in research. I remembered it was before the economic liberation in 1978. We had some practices that were old fashioned, but some practices that were reasonable. At that time, faculty members of common courses were integrated with faculty members of specialized courses. In our teaching and research unit there were specialized faculty members as well as faculty members on math, physics and chemistry. All of us participate in research projects. So through socialization with team members, teaching-only staffs' teaching can be informed by research.

Technological professors like Xu and Shi characterize themselves as free floating molecules who are capable of turning into "new substance" when grouped with other free floating molecules. Shi tells me his experience of being invited to be a statistic analyst to a research team in the Department of Sociology. According to Xu, whether his department can attract funding depends solely on the strength of the research teams formed by faculty members. According to all these stories, teams are the basic units at the university of focus where a great amount work is executed and innovations are initiated and kept on.

In short, Dearlove (2004) states, "universities are both innovative and deeply conservative when it comes to change: Innovative when it comes to piecemeal and incremental change; conservative when it comes to securing support for planned and systemic change across the whole institution" (p. 73). Similarly, Trowler (2002) is making the point that desired and planned change does not necessarily take place while unintended changes frequently prosper at universities. He says that

> [At a university] anything that requires the coordinated effort of the organization in order to start is unlikely to be started. Anything that requires a coordinated effort of the organization in order to be stopped is unlikely to be stopped. (p. 4)

Summary

In Chapter 6, I described inductively the innovations that take place at the university of focus. As these stories spring out of the university people's meaning-making systems and are in harmony with their perceptions of the organizational purposes, these stories are the embodiment of real and concrete organizational changes.

The findings in this chapter suggest that the university of focus is becoming "entrepreneurial" in Clark's (1998) sense. Entrepreneurial activities not only are occurring in the periphery, as Clark hopes, but also have penetrated the academic "heartland" (Slaughter & Rhoades, 2004). The significance of many novel practices is hanging dangling. As innovations do not fit into existing framework of practices, it is difficult to judge whether they create new possibilities, or they jeopardize existing moralities and standards, such as professional identities and academic values. Nevertheless, the university people are negotiating the rules and regulations to their advantage and non-standard practices go on all the time. Freely formed teams and units are the locus where innovative practices are initiated, preserved and disseminate.

Chapter 7
Conclusions and Implications

Summary of the Previous Chapters

In this chapter, I will summarize the findings in the previous chapters, as well as generalize the findings about the university of focus to a broader context, reiterating some of the themes and patterns I have already stated from Chapter 4 to Chapter 6.

The research questions of this research are based on the contradictions and paradoxes in the Chinese neoliberal HE reform policies since 1993. There are tendencies for the Chinese government to pursue economic proficiency while at the same time denying autonomy and self-governance at the university level. That is, the negative sides of neoliberalism tend to be amplified while its romantic goals, such as cultivating local innovations, quality, responsiveness, and differentiation are not attainable. HE reform policies are inevitably top-down and outside-in, as some theorists characterize the mode of Chinese HE reform as "centralized decentralism" or governmental "steering at distance" (Kalsen, 2000; Mok, 2004; Vidovich, 2002; R. Yang et al., 2007).

In this case-study research, I evaluate the implementation or the "situated practices" of the national HE reform policies, the amalgamation, expansion and quality assurance policies, as well as elaborating on the locally-grounded innovative ideas and practices at the university of focus. The methodological approach used is phenomenological interviews, a vehicle that elicits "local knowledge" and accords the status of expertise to the interview participants. The purpose is to map out the different experiences and meanings different social groups (e. g., faculty members, administrators and students) derive from the centralized policies and to generate new ideas for policy actions.

The findings suggest that at the institutional level, the faculty members, administrators, and students are highly reflexive, resilient and pragmatic. Instead of mutely accepting national HE reform policies as given, the university people are making an active effort to reappropriate distant policies, fashioning them into locally meaningful and relevant terms and practices. Furthermore, the findings suggest that small-scale, inside-out innovations grounded in local people's meaning-making systems and in harmony with their perceptions of organizational purposes, profuse and proliferate at the university of focus.

Shore and Wright (1999) note that neoliberal educational policies focus on the Economy and Efficiency rather than Effectiveness of the three "virtuous Es", as they state that

> Civil servants' energy was concentrated on money, time, and staff-saving revisions to internal procedures rather than on larger questions concerning the ultimate effectiveness of programs, their impact on the public and on issues of social justice, and whether their outcomes were consistent with expressed policy aims. (p. 64)

The findings about policy implementation at the university of focus are consistent with Shore and Wright's (1999) comments about neoliberal policies. The university people's experiences with and perceptions of the amalgamation policy concentrate on the group conflict and competition which create winners and losers, and the *de facto* inefficiency and disintegration subsumed by the overpowering official grand discourses on efficiency and economic gains through amalgamation.

Three themes emerge from the analysis of the impacts of the expansion policy on the university people: quality, social justice and disparities among disciplines. First, as the increase in university facilities and resources does not go commensurate with the radical expansion of the student body, the quality of undergraduate education has been placed in constant question. Especially, the expansion not only dilutes resources, but also limits the articulation of quality standards from the "right" channels—frontline faculty members and student consumers whose lives are directly impacted by the expansion. Second, the interviews with the university people concern social equity. Although overall, participants agree about the widening access of university education, sample stories grounded in the personal experiences of faculty members and students suggest that opportunities of college education are more open to the high- but not low-SES students under the expansion conditions. Third, humanities and social sciences disciplines are more vulnerable to the vagaries of the expansion policy, as these disciplines are less well positioned in the national policy discourses on economic development and international integration and in the university's tradition, to compete for resources and support. Moreover, due to the fallacy and pitfalls of the university admission policy, some humanities and social sciences disciplines are facing serious retention and survival problems.

The national quality assurance mechanisms have two layers of impacts on the university people: a direct impact and an impact through co-opting university normal functions and turning them into stretched arms of bureaucratic surveillance and control. I not only analyze the university people's direct experiences with and perceptions of the two rounds of national undergraduate teaching evaluation in November 2007 and April 2008, but also unravel how they react to and reconstitute the extended influence of national quality assurance mechanisms, the *Dudao* Team and faculty promotion policies. The university people display a high degree of "political reflexivity" and resilience. Instead of mutely accepting these mechanisms as given, they either critically unravel the hidden agendas embedded, or mobilize multiple resources to turn them into locally relevant terms and practices.

The analysis on the "situated practices" of national HE reform policies suggests that the "implementation gap" exists between policymaking and enforcement in contextualized sites. Yanow (2002) argues that policies are "authored texts" coded with policymakers' intentions and goals, while through the implementation, the "authored texts" are reconstructed, as policy-relevant groups derive from them "variant and even incommensurable meanings" (p. 9). The purpose of policy implementation or evaluation analysis is to assess the derived meanings against the policy intent, so as to map out the architecture of different "meaning communities" surrounding a policy and to generate new ideas for policy actions. The analysis in this case-study research suggests that the neoliberal encodings in the amalgamation, expansion and quality assurance mechanisms are subject to recoding and reconstruction by social groups who are directly impacted by these policies. Gergen (1992) argues that once given, or stipulated, managerial fiats become the "properties of the community." The findings confirm Gergen and Trolwer's (2002) assertion that policies are "crude and simple" while contextualized practices are "sophisticated, contingent, complex and unstable" (p. 16). Newton (2002) makes similar comments on the "situated factors" and "context" that subvert or distort top-down policies in his evaluation of the national policy implementation at UK universities.

▶ Chapter 7　Conclusions and Implications

  The success in application of a system or definition may be dependent less on the rigor of application or the neatness or theoretical compactness of the 'dry,' documented quality system *per se*, important though that may be, and more on its contingent use by actors, and on how the system is viewed and interpreted by them. (p. 48)

  In addition to evaluating the implementation of the amalgamation, expansion, and quality assurance mechanisms at the university of focus, I invite the university people to reflect upon and narrate instances of "innovations." Universities change through inner debates as well as through passive adaptation to external transitions (e. g., the economy or policies) (Fairwheather, 1996). Reflecting upon and narrating examples of innovations externalizes the university people's "tacit knowledge" and brings their ideas in shape through organizing them into a plot for the sake of an outsider (Kaplan, 1986; Nonaka, 1994). The incidences the university people tell about innovations are grounded in the localized meaning-making systems and in harmony with their perceptions of the organizational purposes, and therefore, are the embodiment of genuine inside-out organizational changes.

  I describe inductively the five properties of innovative incidences. There is a "wild profusion" of innovative ideas and practices in every nook and cranny of the university of focus, just as Button (2003) states that innovations are often found in the "unexpected" places in the organization. The idea on "entrepreneurialism" and "academic capitalism" profuse and proliferate at the university level. Although such phenomena are more criticized and negatively viewed elsewhere (American Council on Education, n. d., Slaughter & Rhoades, 2004; Trowler, 2001; Geiger, 2004; Marginson & Considine, 2000), they are more warmly perceived and received at the university of focus. The innovative ideas and practices in the local faculty members, administrators and students' perspectives are ambiguous, unstable, team-based and resistant to institutionalization. The vitality and dynamism in local innovations provide an alternative to top-down and outside-in efforts to change the university.

Implications

Having summarized the major findings of this case-study research, my next task is to discuss why the findings about a single university are relevant to the broader context. According to Tatkirm et al. (1997), critical policy research is "interested not only in what is going on and why, but also in doing something about it" (p. 38). This research not only is a description of the policy implementation and local university innovations, but also has "praxis" embedded in it, that is, I try to make suggestions for policy actions. Given the high-level of reconstructions and resistance towards the national HE reform policies at the university of focus as well as the "wild profusion" of localized innovative ideas and practices at the university, I first highlight the idiosyncratic nature of university organizations vis-à-vis other types of organizations (e.g., business corporation, annexations to government bureaus) and then I propose alternative models to policymaking, with attendant attention to policy analysts' role in the policy process.

The nature of university organizations

It is important for high-level leaders in educational bureaus and at universities to recognize the distinctions between the university organizations and other types of organizations (e.g., governmental bureaus, business corporations). There is a tendency, in the Chinese social-political traditions, for universities to be viewed as annexations of governmental bureaus (Bastid, 1987; Hayhoe,

1996; Pepper, 1996). In the compelling discourse of neoliberal economic globalization, a new set of conceptions that view universities as business corporations are laid on top of the Chinese traditions. In this context, "policy is formulated by management and decisions flow down through middle-level managers to the floor. The emphasis is on quantifiable objectives, clear role specifications and the testing of the implementation of the objectives by performance indictors" (Boer, 1996). Although business corporations have largely abandoned those ideas on line-management (Trolwer, 1998), in HE, however, the classic management concept is becoming more popular and influential. Even some scholars unquestioningly equate universities with other types of organizations in their scholarly research (W. S. Chen, 2002; Y. M. Wan, 2008).

The findings of this research suggest just the contrary. Universities display many of the loosely-coupled, bottom-heavy or organized-anarchical characteristics (Cohen & March, 1986; Weick, 1976). Levin (2006) further describes a university as full of antagonist cultures and Houston (2008) refers to a university as a "mess" which has to answer to multiple stakeholders who have different and often contradictory expectations of the functions of universities. The findings display that the university of focus is a multivocal, heteroglossia and polysemic site; universities are milieus of contesting, negotiating, reconstructing, displacing and creating discourses, so as to significantly undermine the constitutive power of a single hegemonic discourse (e.g., neoliberalism). The original purposes of policies and outcomes do not necessarily match, as distant national policies are owned and re-appropriated dynamically by people down the educational line.

This confirms Trowler's (2001) analysis of the managerial discourses at universities in the United Kingdom. Although it might be threatening and impending elsewhere, the managerial ideology not only faces competing structures but also individual agency that rises out of the activity systems (e. g. , academic departments) and the communities of practices (e. g. , research groups) in a university context. For instance, conditioning structures like different educational ideologies (e. g. , traditionalism, enterprise, progressivism and social reconstructionism) and norms vested in different disciplines, will either enhance or mitigate the managerialist discourse, depending on if the existing educational ideologies are aligned with or conflictual to managerialism. Furthermore, individuals and groups interpret and create meanings on a moment-to-moment basis as they "work together on the issues of professional life" (p. 194), so as to challenge and alter existing structures.

In other words, decisions made on the basis of the bureaucratic or corporate perceptions of universities tend to be subverted and resisted. The amalgamation, expansion, and quality assurance policies are generated in governmental bureaus and highly centralized. They attempt to project the "industrial process" (technical-rational planning and reforms) onto the universities (Weick, 1976) and thus encounter high-degree of resistance and reconstitution. Reform efforts should be centered around the natural "state of being" of the universities and be less ambitious, small-scale and bottom-up (Clark, 1983, 1998). Top-down or bottom-up decision-making is not up to the choice of people inside and outside of universities; the way a university should be reformed and managed is built into its very structure.

Ruth Simmons, the president of Brown University, provides an ideal version of the government-university relationship that the universities should have "as little interference from the State as possible. The role of the State is to provide resources but to give wide latitude to university leaders to decide how scholarship is to advance" (Simmons, 2003). The same would be held true for university leaders in their relationship to middle-level academic leaders like deans and department heads: provide resources but exert little interference. High-level leaders in governmental bureaus and at universities should keep in mind the organizational model of universities as bottom heavy, loosely-coupled, and organized anarchic, so that false attempts to reform universities top-down and outside-in which are time-consuming and wasteful of resources, can be avoided.

Besides resistance towards top-down policies, the findings in this study suggest that innovations are locally grounded, resistant to institutionalization, and are negotiated on a day-to-day, face-to-face basis. In other words, departments and colleges, and administrative sections, the "activity systems" of the universities are at the same time the locus for small-scale, local innovations to be initiated and developed. Self-organizing teams are likely to be formed at this level to carry out the basic functions of the university (e.g., teaching and research) through which innovative ideas and practices are most likely to sparkle and spread. Middle-level academic leaders should consider how they can facilitate the formation of self-organizing teams and the initiation and spread of innovations at the local level.

Information channels should be open between middle-level academic leaders and administrators and the ordinary organization members. A leader's role, according to Lueddeke (1999), is not to impose standard behaviors on people, but focuses on "the uncovering of meaning that is already embedded in other's minds, helping them to see what they already know, believe, and value and encouraging them to make new meaning" (p. 237). When the means of communication between ordinary members and their immediate leaders are structurally blocked, the ordinary members, according to Chiper (2007), will

> Act as self filters and by assuming a too large psychological distance, they prevent solutions from being found and thus perpetuate the status quo. The lack of communication between leadership and followers makes

room for the proliferation of small talk, rumors and gossip. Lack of information will breed misinformation, and too little 'talk'...will create too much 'small talk' which can be detrimental to the institution's image and desired atmosphere of trust and transparency. (p. 721)

Thus, regular storytelling workshops are suggested to be held at the departmental and college levels to elicit "counter stories" to managerial account in order to challenge outmoded ways of working, diagnose barriers to intentional change, or tap new ideas on practices (Rhodes & Brown, 2005). Storytelling becomes a mode of communication and empowerment tool for ordinary members.

Sometimes, there is a tendency for university people, especially the faculty members and students, to be passively resisting when policies or other discourses are in opposition to their interests or well-beings. For instance, faculty members in the study sometimes keep academic leaders and non-academic administrators at arm's length when the former's norms and discourses are in contention with the latter's. Faculty members tend to mind only their own businesses, but not make active efforts to enter their stories and opinions to the more public sphere. Students sometimes do not exercise their consumer rights, but passively accept what is given by the policy discourses, out of fear, disillusion, or habitual passivity. Although in this research, I have made some efforts to amplify the voices of socially disenfranchised groups such as students and faculty members, further channels need to be open in order that faculty members' and students' views and stories can enter the broader and public sphere.

Alternative models on policymaking and policy analysts' role

The technical-rational or "staircase" model of policymaking prevails in the centralized, top-down policy process of Chinese HE reforms. This model, bearing particular assumptions, excludes the representation of wider, more participatory voices from the below, especially the voices of those on which the policies have a direct impact. A more participatory model needs to be created so that Habermas' "communication rationality" could be realized (deLeon & deLeon, 2002a), in which a policy analyst may play a constructive role so as to bring out the positive outcomes.

The traditional technical rational model of policymaking (Trowler, 2002) breaks policy process into several independent cycles, each with distinct beginning and end: policy formation (that includes definition of problem, generating policy alternatives and making selections) and policy implementation. It is assumed if each step of policymaking is guarded by scientific, objective, uninterested data, then the natural corollary is that the outcome of policy implementation will match the original policy intentions and purposes. First, reality (problems) is conceptualized as "out there" to be discovered and acted upon. Policy researchers/makers are to glean the data about reality, and formulate a few policy alternatives until finally settling down with a policy object on the basis of empirical evidence. Second, the policy is to be implemented in order to alter the problematic situation. If the data pertaining to social reality, and the judgment criteria of policy alternatives are objective, value-neutral and collected through "scientific" methodologies, and if the policy objectives are clearly stated and faithfully implemented, there should be no question that the social situation be altered, if not necessarily ameliorated, according to the policy actors' intention and design. Stone (2002) comments that in this model, "policy is regarded as being created in a fairly orderly sequence of stages, almost as if on an assembly line" (p.11).

In this technical-rational model, technocrats' expertise is trusted into the central position, while the larger public is left out on the basis of lacking specialized knowledge. Fischer (1990) broadly classifies three groups in national policymaking: (a) a top echelon of political and economic elites, (b) a technocratic echelon of experts/applied scientists and specialized administrators, and (c) a large depoliticized mass public. As technocrat concepts have acquired primacy in modern society, the discourses of experts trained in "applied sciences," their languages (e.g., modes of argument and theories) are often privileged over that of the general public. Experts' opinions unusually lend power to legitimacy and support the decisions of top political leaders. Therefore, the top echelons of the society, the technical experts and political elites, form "discourse coalitions" to the degree that excludes the general mass, on the basis of the latter's lack of knowledge. The ordinary people are often portrayed as "needy" or "socially disadvantaged" without their perspectives being presented in the public policy discourses, although they might occasionally get involved as survey or interview subjects. Fischer's characterization of the centralized, top-down policies applies to the Chinese national HE reform policies: the amalgamation, expansion and quality assurance mechanisms, given the overreliance on technocrat experts' knowledge and the political leaders' central role in setting these policies in motion. The argument made in support of centralized policymaking is that "poorly informed, "inadequately coordinated actions would be replaced by knowledgeable planning, adaptation, and policy development" (McLendon, Heller & Young, 2005, p. 364; see also Kang, 2000).

Among many opponents of the technical-rational model of policymaking, are supporters of an alternative political-rational model in which social process is characterized as an endless struggle for power and control by different social groups (Tatkirm et al. 1997). People's understanding of reality or the "problem" is no longer unified and objective, but deeply ingrained in the values, perceptions, and interests of different social groups. Policy development is therefore both "a continuous and a contested process in which those with competing values and differential access to power seek to form and shape policy in their own interests" (Bell & Stevenson, 2006).

According to the proponents of the political-rational model of policymaking, social policies are inevitably contested and by no means are able to achieve unitary results, as Ginsburg et al. (1990) state that "what some people see as constructive change, others may perceive as either tokenism or destructive or regressive change" (pp. 446 – 447). Hosking (2006), seeing centralized policymaking as the privileged discourses imposing themselves on and marginalizing competing views, anticipates that resistance will be inevitable. Malen (2006) draws the same conclusion, although based on different reasons. Through empirical findings, he argues that, as there are inevitable mismatch between different speech communities, it is likely that centralized policies are distorted and misinterpreted, as the language of top policy-makers cannot be translated into that of "receivers" without problem. The findings in this case-study research support such claims given the high-degree of reconstitution and reconstruction of the national HE reform policies at the ground level.

Thus political-rational model tends to demerit top-down policymaking and enforcement, given the potentials of the imposition of the priorities and values of one social group on other groups. According to Fischer (1990), the policymaking process is naturally full of group competition, bargain and compromises. It is not like the neat, and monolithic technical-experts based process, which, as deLeon & deLeon (2002a, 2002b) describe, is achieved through "systematically distorted communications," in which "one party or coalition (e.g., interest groups or governmental agencies) has a clear and persistent dominance in a policy arena over other relevant parties and consistently avails itself of that authority" (p. 482). When the policymaking process is too consensual, and too few arguments are presented concerning a complex policy problem, we need to start to worry. Alternative policymaking, aiming to achieve individual self-actualization, needs to present the voices of as many people as possible. Those at the "receive end" of policies, given the systematic suppression and silencing of their voices in policy discourses, are in dire need of being amplified. Thus, in political-rational model of policymaking, it is advocated that opinions and views from those who constitute the "receive end" need to be recruited. More utilitarian argument sees recruiting voices from the "receive end" as precluding resistance, while more utopian view maintains that it is a means to widening participation.

Malen (2006), for instance, suggests that either before the generation of policies, or during the implementation, policymakers and "receivers" should come to conversation in order to familiarize each other's languages. In the same fashion, Rein and Schön (1993, 1996; see also Schön & Rein, 1994) are making a strong case that policy makers, implementers and analysts should listen to views and opinions at the receive end in order to engage in "frame-reflection." To them, when policy actors have developed more personal relations with, or when they have accepted the stories of the "receivers," policy actors are more likely to reflect on their own limitations, develop "double visions" and engage in the solution of intractable policy controversies.

The political-rational model of policymaking poses challenges for the role of policy analysts, either in "analysis of policy" (post policy evaluation) or "analysis for policy" (collecting information before the generation of policy objects) (Tatkirm et al., 1997).

First, policy analysts no longer assume the detached, uninterested role outside of the process. Instead, policy analysts focus on "local" knowledge which involves values, beliefs and feelings (Yanow, 1996, 2002; 2006). Rein and Schön (1993, 1996; see also Schön & Rein, 1996) argue that each interest group is ingrained in certain "policy frame" which is a way of "selecting, organizing, interpreting and making sense of a complex reality to provide guidance for knowing, analyzing, persuading and acting. A frame is a perspective from which an amorphous, ill-defined, problematic situation can be made sense of and acted on" (Rein & Schön, 1993, p. 146). In order to access these frames that are sources of intractable policy disputes and controversies, policy analysts, in the process of research, need to accord the status of expertise to the researched, as the latter have epistemological advantages and know their own lifeworlds and experiences. The analysts need to assume a "sustained empathetic" attitude in listening to the views and stories of the researched.

Second, the analysts need to "demystify" their own discourse location. The political-rational model of policymaking recognizes the analysts as "already embedded practitioners" who, coming out of the educational credentialing process, use "standards of judgment, canons of evidence or normative measures" that anchor to certain communities of practices (Dodge, Ospina & Foldy, 2005). Rein and Schön (1993, 1996) encourage policy analysts to engage in "frame" reflection. Fischer (1990) maintaines that the "technical expertise" like policy analysts' technical languages serves to set the deliberative framework, and justify policy choices of political leaders to an extent that depoliticize the larger mass. Without recognizing the hidden ideologies embedded in professional languages and theories and modes of argumentation, policy analysts are "letting the prevailing power structure to play ventriloquist. When they let the existing structure of domination speak through their mouths, the alternative policy responses proffered for meeting 'the situation' are predetermined by the interests that constitute 'the situation' to begin with" (Danziger, 1995, p. 440).

Third, the policy analysts need to not only form, but also help those contending policy-related groups, especially those policy elites (e. g. , top political leaders) form "double vision." "Double vision" is a term Schön and Rein (1994) borrow from Lisa Bettie, which they define as "the ability to act from one perspective while, in the back of our minds, we hold onto an awareness of other possible perspectives" (p. xvii). Forming "double vision" means coming out of the insulation and narrowness of one's own mental frame, conventions, and habits of practices, and learning/ understanding other people's situation, so as to achieve a consensus or what Habermas terms as "communicative rationality." Stubborn controversies are given rise to while each contending groups are ensconced in their separated frames. "Double vision" enables them to not only act, but also exam the "frames" from which they act (instead of taking them for granted). With "double vision", the involving groups are able to enter the frames of other actors. Once the hidden "frames" operating behind the scenes are demystified and exposed, a possibility of mutual understanding can be achieved. Moreover, "reframing" is in prospect—there is a promise of solving the policy controversy.

In short, this case-study research draws heavily from policy scientists like Yanow (1996, 2002, 2006) and Rein and Schön (1993, 1994, see also Schön & Rein, 1996), and partially achieves the goals as outlined above: (a) tapping the experiential knowledge of the university people that involves feelings, values and beliefs, (b) reflecting upon the researcher's positionality, (c) mapping out and compare different "communities of meanings," so that each community is able to access the meaning other groups derive from the national HE reform policies. More research following this line of analysis needs to be conducted in searching for mitigating the negative impact of top-down, centralized policies, resolving stubborn and intractable conflicts and achieving a lifeworld in Habermas' sense.

References

Alsup, J. (2004). Protean subjectivities: Qualitative research and the inclusion of the personal. In S. G. Brown & S. I. Dobrin (Eds.). *Ethnography unbound: from theory shock to critical praxis* (pp. 219-237). Albany: State University of New York Press.

Altbach, P. G. (1981). The university as center and periphery. *Teachers College Record*, 82 (4), 601-621.

Altbach, P. G. (2001). Gigantic peripheries: India and China in the international knowledge system. In R. Hayhoe & J. Pan (Eds.). *Knowledge across cultures: A contribution to dialogue among civilizations* (pp. 199 - 214). Hong Kong, China: Comparative Research Education Center.

Altbach, P. G. (2004). Globalization and the university: Myths and realities in an unequal world. *Tertiary Education and Management*, 10, 3-25.

Altheide, D. (1987). Ethnographic content analysis. *Qualitative Sociology*, 10, 65-77.

American Council on Education (n. d.). The brave new (and smaller) world of higher education: Transatlantic view. Retrieved June 13, 2007 from http://www.eua.be/fileadmin/user_upload/files/EUA1_documents/brave-new-world.1069322743534.pdf

Argyris, C. (1993). *Knowledge for action: A guide overcoming barriers to organizational change*. San Francisco: Jossey-Bass.

Askling, B., & Stensaker, B. (2000). Academic leadership: Prescriptions, practices and paradoxes. *Tertiary Education and*

Management, 8 (2), 113 – 125.

Atkinson, R. (1998). *The life story interview.* Thousand Oaks, CA: Sage.

Baker, M. (2007, November 17). China's bid for world domination. BBC news. Retrieved September 5, 2009, from http://news.bbc.co.uk/2/hi/uk_news/education/7098561.stm

Bao, R., & Liu, R. (2002). Governmental support or competing in the market: Commenting on the external environment of university development. *Journal of Beijing Institute of Technology*, 4 (1), 70 – 73.

Barnett, R. (2000). *Realizing the University in an Age of Supercomplexity.* Buckingham, UK: The Society for Research into Higher Education and Open University.

Barrows, L. C. (2001). Higher education institutions and their regions: Linking the local and the global. *Higher Education in Europe*, XXVI (3), 305 – 314.

Barry, M. (1999). Control of education: Issues and tensions in centralization and decentralization. In R. F. Arnove & C. A. Torres (Eds.). *Comparative education: The dialectic of the global and the local* (pp. 207 – 232). Lanham, MD: Rowman & Littlefield.

Bastid, M. (1987). Servitude or liberation: The introduction of foreign educational practices and systems to China from 1840 to the present. In R. Hayhoe & M. Bastid (Eds.). *China's education and the industrialized world: Studies in cultural transfer* (pp. 3 – 20). New York: M. E. Sharpe.

Bell, L., & Stevenson, H. (2006). *Education policy: Process, themes and impact.* New York: Routledge.

Boje, D. M. (2001). *Narrative methods for organizational and communication research.* London: Sage.

Boer, H. D. (1996). Changing institutional governance structures. In P. A. M. Maassen & F. A. Van Vught (eds.). *Inside academia: New challenges for the academic profession* (pp. 83 – 96). Utrecht, the Netherlands: Center for Higher Education Policy Studies.

Brennan, J., & Shah, T. (2000a). Quality assessment and institutional change: Experiences from 14 countries. *Higher Education*, *40*, 331 – 349.

Brennan, J., & Shah, T. (2000b). *Managing quality in higher education: An international perspective on institutional assessment and change*. Philadelphia: OECD SRHE and Open University Press.

Bridgman, T. (2007). Freedom and autonomy in the university enterprise. *Journal of Organizational Change*, *20* (4), 478 – 490.

Button, J. (2003). Breathing life into organizational studies. *Journal of Management Inquiry*, *12* (1), 5 – 19.

Campbell, T. I. D., & Slaughter, S. (1999). Faculty and administrators' attitudes towards potential conflicts of interest, commitment and equity in university-industry relationships. *The Journal of Higher Education*, *70* (3), 309 – 352.

Chen, B., & Yuan, Z. W. (2000). Tentative argument on the meaning of the phrase "enhancing the macro-controlling power of the provincial government over the universities". *Higher Education Exploration*, *3*, 28 – 32.

Chen, D. Y. (2002). The amalgamation of Chinese higher education institutions. *Education Policy Analysis Archives*, *10* (20).

Chen, W. S. (2002). *Personnel decisions in public institutions: The choice over personnel decisions at Chinese universities at a time of radical change*. China: Henan People's Publishing House.

Chen, X. F. (2006). Policymaking guided by ideal models. *Beijing University Education Review*, *4* (1), 145 – 157.

Chiper, S. (2006). The discourse of Romanian universities. *Journal of Organizational Change*, *19* (6), 713 – 724.

Clark, B. R. (1983). *The higher education system: Academic organization in cross-national perspective*, Berkeley, CA: University of California Press.

Clark, B. R. (1996). Substantive growth and innovative organization: New categories for higher education research. *Higher Education, 32* (4), 417–430.

Clark, B. R. (1998). *Creating entrepreneurial universities: Organizational pathways of transformation*. New York: Pergamon.

Cohen, M. D., & March, J. G. (1986). *Leadership and ambiguity* (2nd ed.). Boston: Harvard Business School Press.

Corwin, R. G. (1974). Models of educational organizations. *Review of Research in Education, 2*, 247–295.

Crabtree, F., & Miller, W. (1999). *Doing qualitative research* (2nd ed.). Thousand Oaks, CA: Sage.

Curran, T. D. (2005). *Educational reform in republican China: The failure of educators to create a modern nation*. New York: The Edwin Mellen.

Czarniawska, B. (1998). *A narrative approach to organization studies*. Thousand Oaks, CA: Sage.

Danziger, M. (1995). Policy analysis postmodernized: Some political and pedagogical ramifications. *Policy Studies Journal, 23* (3), 435–450.

Darling-Hammond, L. (1990). Instructional policy into practice: "The power of the bottom over the top". *Educational Evaluation and Policy Analysis, 12*, 339–347.

Dearlove, J. (1998). The deadly dull issue of university "administration?" Good governance, managerialism and organizing academic work. *Higher Education Policy, 11*, 59–79.

Deetz, S. (1992). *Democracy in an age of corporate colonization: Developments in communication and politics of everyday*. Albany: State of New York University Press.

deLeon, L., & deLeon, P. (2002a). The democratic ethos and public management. *Administration and Society*, *34* (2), 229–250.

deLeon, P. & deLeon, L. (2002b). Whatever happened to policy implementation? An alternative approach. *Journal of Public Administration Research and Theory*, *12* (4), 467–492.

Delany, B., & Paine, L. W. (1991). Shifting patterns of authority in Chinese schools. *Comparative Education Review*, *35* (1), 23–43.

Dill, D. D. (1997). Accreditation, assessment, anarchy? The evolution of academic quality assurance policies in the United States. In J. Brennan (Ed.). *Standards and quality in higher education* (pp. 15–43). London: Jessica Kingsley.

Dill, D. D. (2003). An institutional perspective on higher education policy: The case of academic quality assurance. In J. C. Smart (Ed.). *Higher education: Handbook of theory and research* (Vol. 18, pp. 669–695). Norwell, MA: Kluwer Academic.

Ding, A., & Levin, J. S. (2007). The interventionary state in China and programs and curricula at a Chinese vocational university. *Higher Education*, *53*, 539–560.

Ding, X. H., & Chen, L. K. (2000). On the impact of university expansion on economic growth and increase of employment opportunity. *Research in Educational Development*, *2*, 9–14.

Ding, X. H., & Min, W. F. (1997). The economy of scale and the restructuring of higher education. *Journal of Higher Education*, *2*, 1–8.

Dodge, J., Ospina, S. M., Foldy, E. G. (2005). Integrating rigor and relevance in pubic administration scholarship: The contribution of narrative inquiry. *Public Administration Review*, *65* (3), 286–300.

Dong, Y. C. (2004). *On the relationship between Chinese universities, government and society*. China: Yunnan University

Press.

Dong, Y. C. (2005). *In search for the ideas on university*. China: Yunnan University Press.

Doyle, W. & Ponder, G. A. (1977). The practicality ethnic in teacher decision-making. *Interchange*, 8 (3), 1 – 12.

Drake, E. (2001). World Bank transfer of technology and ideas to India and China. In R. Hayhoe & J. Pan (Eds.). *Knowledge across cultures: A contribution to dialogue among civilizations* (pp. 215 – 228). Hong Kong, China: Comparative Research Education Center.

Erickson, F. (1986). Qualitative methods in research on teaching. In M. Wittrock. (Ed.), *Handbook of research on teaching* (3rd ed.) (pp. 119 – 161). New York: Macmillan.

Etzkowitz, H., Webster, A., Gebhardt, C., & Terra, B. R. C. (2000). The future of the university and the university of the future: Evolution of ivory tower to entrepreneurial paradigm. *Research Policy*, 29, 313 – 330.

Fairweather, J. S. (1996). *Faculty work and public trust: Restoring the value of teaching and public service in American academic life*. Needham Heights, MA: Allyn & Bacon.

Fenstermacher, G. D. & Soltis, J. F. (2004). *Approaches to teaching*. New York: Teachers' College Press.

Finch, J. (1997). Power, legitimacy and academic standards. In J. Brennan (Ed.). *Standards and quality in higher education* (pp. 146 – 156). London: Jessica Kingsley.

Findlow, S. (2008). Accountability and innovation in higher education: A disabling tension? *Studies in Higher Education*, 33 (3), 313 – 329.

Fischer, F. (1990). *Technocracy and the politics of expertise*. London: Sage.

Fox, R., & Fox, J. (2004). *Organizational discourse: A language-ideology-power perspective*. Westport, CT: London.

Gabriel, Y. (1995). The unmanaged organization: Stories, fantasies, and subjectivity. *Organization Studies*, *16*, 477 - 501.

Gabriel, Y. (1998). The use of stories. In G. Symon & C. Cassell (Eds.). *Qualitative methods and analysis in organizational research: A practical guide* (pp. 135 - 160). London: Sage.

Gamage, D. T. (1992) Recent reforms in Australian higher education with particular reference to institutional amalgamations. *Higher Education*, *24* (1), 77 - 92.

Gamage, D. T. (1993). The reorganization on the Australian higher education institutions towards a unified national system. *Studies in Higher Education*, *18* (1), 81 - 94.

Gan, D. A., & Wan, L. L. (2005). The change of the belongings of higher education and governmental role. *Modern Education Science*, *2*, 18 - 21.

Gao, G. J. (2001). Does the amalgamation of flagship universities leads to world-class status: A reflection on the amalgamation of flagship universities in our country. *Heilongjiang Research on Higher Education*, *3*, 9 - 10.

Gao, R. S. (2007). The reflections on the development of science and technology at universities in a new century. In Z. G. Yuan (Ed.). *Review on Chinese Educational Policies* (pp. 12 - 20). Beijing, China: Education Science Publishing House.

Geiger, R. L. (2004). *Knowledge and money: Research universities and the paradox of the marketplace*. CA: Stanford University Press.

Gergen, K. J. (1992). Organization theory in the postmodern era. In M. Reed & M. Hughes (Eds.). *Rethinking organization: New directions in organization theory and analysis* (pp. 207 - 226). London: Sage.

Ginsburg, M. B., Cooper, S., Raghu, R., & Zegarra, H.

(1990). National and world-system explanation of educational reform. *Comparative Education Review*, *34* (4), 474 – 499.

Goedegebuure, L. C. J. (1992). *Mergers in higher education: A comparative perspective*. Utrecht, the Netherlands: Lemma.

Gopinatha, S., & Altbach, P. G. (2005). Rethinking centre-perihery. *Asian Pacific Journal of Education*, *25* (2), 117 – 123.

Gornitzka, A., Larsen, I. M. (2004). Towards professionalization? Restructuring of administrative work force in universities. *Higher Education*, *47*, 455 – 471.

Gornitzka, A., Kogan, M., Amaral, A. (2005). Introduction. In A. Gornitzka, M. Kogan, & A. Amaral (Eds.). *Reform and change in higher education: Analyzing policy implementation* (pp. 1 – 14). Dordrecht, the Netherlands: Springer.

Gornitzka, A., Kyvik, S., & Stensaker, B. (2005). Implementation analysis in higher education. In A. Gornitzka, M. Kogan, & A. Amaral (Eds.). *Reform and change in higher education: Analyzing policy implementation* (pp. 35 – 56). Dordrecht, The Netherlands: Springer.

Green, A. (1997). *Education, globalization and the nation state*. London: MacMillan.

Green, A. (1999). Education and globalization in Europe and East Asia: Convergent and divergent trends. *Journal of Educational Policy*, *14* (1), 55 – 71.

Gu, K. F. (2006, March 20). Education, aged-care service and housing are the three motivations for citizens to save. *Consumption Daily*, p. A04.

Gu, H. B., & Wang, B. Y. (2004, April). The evaluation systems of science and technological research in China and foreign countries: Comparisons and suggestions on improvement. *China Opening Journal*, *2*, 74 – 100.

Guba, E., & Lincoln, Y. (1994). Competing paradigms in qualitative research. In N. K. Denzin & Y. S. Lincoln (Eds.). *Handbook of qualitative research* (pp. 105 – 117). Thousand Oaks, CA: SAGE.

Gumport, P. (2000). Academic restructuring: Organizational change and institutional imperatives. *Higher Education*, *39*, 67 – 91.

Guo, G. Y. (1998). A rational analysis on university amalgation. *Journal of Higher Education*, *2*, 33 – 37.

Han, Y. X., Weng, J., & Zhou, B. (2007). Chinese undergraduates' decisions on and expectations of careers: Using Zhejiang province as an example. *Chinese Journal of Population Science*, *3*, 63 – 71.

Hanson, E. M. (1997). Strategies of educational decentralization: Key questions and core issues. *Journal of Educational Administration*, *36* (2), 111 – 128.

Harman, G. (2000). Institutional mergers in Australian higher education. *Higher Education Quarterly*, *54* (4), 343 – 366.

Hartnett, R. A. (1998). *The saga of Chinese higher education from the Tongzhi Restoration to Tiananmen Square: Revolution and reform.* Lewiston, NY: The Edwin Mellen.

Harvey, L., & Newton, J. (2004). Transforming quality evaluation. *Quality in Higher Education*, *10* (2), 150 – 165.

Hawkins, J. (2000). Centralization, decentralization, recentralization: Education reform in China. *Journal of Educational Administration*, *38* (5), 442 – 454.

Hayhoe, R. (1996). *China's universities*, 1895 – 1995: *A century of cultural conflict.* New York: Garland.

Henkel, M. (2000). *Academic identities and policy change in higher education.* London: Jessica Kingsley.

Hertz, R. (1997). Introduction: Reflexivity and voice. In R. Hertz (Ed.). *Reflexivity and voice* (pp. vii – xvii). Thousand Oaks, CA: Sage.

Hoecht, A. (2006). Quality assurance in UK higher education: Issues of trust, control, professional autonomy and accountability. *Higher Education*, *51*, 541 – 563.

Hosking, D. M. (2006). Organization, organizing, and related concepts of change. In D. M. Hosking, & S. McNamee, (Eds.) *The social construction of organization* (pp. 54 – 69). Herndon, VA: Liber & Copenhagen Business School Press.

Houston, D. (2008). Rethinking quality and improvement in higher education. *Quality Assurance in Education*, *16* (1), 61 – 79.

Huang, F. (2005). Qualitative enhancement and quantitative growth: Changes and trends of China's higher education. *Higher Education Policy*, *18*, 117 – 130.

Jacobson, H. K., & Oksenberg, M. (1990). *China's participation in the IMF, the World Bank, and GATT: Toward a global economic order*. Ann Arbor: University of Michigan Press.

Jiang, Z. M. (1999, June 15). Speech at the third national meeting on educational work. Retrieved April 28, 2010 from http://www.sxu.edu.cn/student/fivestar/starfire/zhuyi/dxptheory/ziliao/6.htm

Jones, P. W. (2007). *World Bank financing of education: Leading, learning and development* (2nd ed.). London: Routledge.

Kalsen, G. E. (2000). Decentralized centralism: Framework for a better understanding of governance in the field of education. *Journal of Educational Policy*, *15* (5), 525 – 538.

Kang, N. (2000). On educational decisions and innovative policies: Using the 1999 policies on university expansions as an example, *Joural of Higher Education*, *2*, 31 – 38.

Kang, N. (2005). The characteristics of resource distribution for higher education at a turning period in our country. In Z. G. Yuan (Ed.) *Review on Chinese education policies* (pp. 142 – 178). Beijing, China: Education Science Publishing House.

Kaplan, T. J. (1986). The narrative structure of policy analysis.

Journal of Policy Analysis and Management, 5 (4), 761 – 778.

Karlsson, G. (1993). Psychological qualitative research from a phenomenological perspective. Stockholm, Sweden: Almqvist & Wiksell.

Kells, H. R. (1999). National higher education evaluation systems: Methods for analysis and some propositions for the research and policy void. *Higher Education*, 38, 209 – 232.

Kerr, C. (1972). *The uses of university*. Cambridge, MA: Harvard University Press.

Krucken, G. (2009). Learning the "new, new thing": On the role of path dependency in university structures. *Higher Education*, 46 (3), 315 – 339.

Lai, D. S. (2004). On the impact of human-capital investments on the unemployment of university graduates. *Beijing University Education Review*, 14, 13 – 15.

Lai, D. S., & Tian, Y. B. (2005). An explanation on the educated unemployment in China. *Economic Studies*, 11, 111 – 119.

Lai, D. S., & Tian, Y. B. (2009). The reason for the unemployment of college graduates and policy solutions. *Red Flag Manuscript*, 7, 34 – 36.

Law, W. W. (1996). Fortress state, cultural continuities and economic change: Higher education in mainland China and Taiwan. *Comparative Education*, 32 (3), 377 – 393.

Levin, J. S. (2006). Faculty work: Tension between educational and economic values. *The Journal of Higher Education*, 77 (1), 62 – 88.

Li, F. L., Morgan, W. J., & Ding, X. H. (2008). The expansion of higher education, employment and over-education in China. *International Journal of Educational Development*, 28, 687 – 697.

Li, F. L., Ding, X. H., & Morgan, W. J. (2009). Higher education and the starting wages of graduate in China.

International Journal of Educational Development, 29, 374 – 381.

Li, J. (2009). Fostering citizenship in China's move from elite to mass higher education: An analysis of students' political socialization and civic participation. *International Journal of Educational Development*, 29, 382 – 398.

Li, J., & Yan, Y. C. (2008). From controlling to serving: The changing of government role in our country higher education appraisal. *Higher Education Daily*, 26 (1), 36 – 38.

Li, J. F., & Guo, P. (2004). The financial policy for China's mass education and its reform. *Education on Economics*, 4, 39 – 43.

Li, L. Q. (2000, August, 25). A report on the strategy of revitalizing the national through science and technology. *Guanging Daily*, Retrieved April 28, 2010, from http://www.gmw.cn/01gmrb/2000-08/25/GB/08% 5E18523% 5E0% 5EGMA2-205.htm

Li, L. Q. (2003, December 11). Li Lanqing releases the unknown facts about the expansion. *The China Youth Daily*, Retrieved April 28, 2010 from http://www.people.com.cn/GB/jiaoyu/1055/2240170.html

Li, P. (1995, July 15). Develop higher education enterprise through reform. *China Education Daily*, p. 1.

Li, W. L. (2002). On the university expansion and its relations to the supply and demand of financial resources. Retrieved September 4, 2009 from http://www.edu.cn/zong_he_317/20060323/t20060323_26298_3.shtml

Lin, M. Q., Zhou, X. J., & Zhen, X. M. (2005). Start evaluations of "first-grade" disciplines and enhance the improvements of disciplines. *China Higher Education*, 6, 40 – 41.

Lin, Y. C. (2007). On the relationship between educational policies and educational research: A reflection on the university expansion policy. *Education Research and Practice*, 3, 61 – 62.

Lincoln, Y. S. (1983). The structure of promotion and tenure decisions in institutions of higher education: A policy analysis. *The Review of Higher Education, 6* (3), 217 – 231.

Liu, H. Y. (2005). A contrastive analysis on science and technological awards in non-governmental and governmental sectors. *Journal of Taiyuan Teachers' College, 4* (2), 26 – 28.

Liu, N. C., & Liu, L. (2005). University rankings in China. *Higher Education in Europe. 30* (2), 217 – 227.

Lofmark, A., Morberg, A., Ohlund, L., Ilicki, J. (2009). Supervising mentors' lived experience on supervision in teaching, nursing, and social care education: A participation-oriented phenomenological study. *Higher Education, 57*, 107 – 123.

Lock, L. F., Silverman, S. J., & Spirduso, W. (2004). *Reading and understanding research*. Thousand Oaks, CA: Sage.

Lueddeke, G. R. (1999). Toward a constructivist framework for guiding change and innovation in higher education. *The Journal of Higher Education, 70* (3), 235 – 260.

Luo, D. M., & Liu, J. (2008). On the problems of university expansion policies. *Contemporary Education Science, 3*, 24 – 26.

Luo, Y., & Ye, F. G. (2003). The human resource policy reform at Beijing University in 2003: An analysis from the perspective of neo-institutionalism. Retrieved July 6, 2009, from http://www.tecn.cn/data/11188.html

Ma, H. W. (2007). A Chinese style solution to the enrolment expansion. *Openings, 14*, 20 – 23.

Ma, Y., & Qin, Y. (2008). An economic analysis on undergraduates' job market against a background of university expansion. *Modern Economic Science, 30* (2), 53 – 58.

Malen, B. (2006). Language matters: How characteristics of language complicate policy implementation. In M. I. Honig

(Ed.). *New directions in education policy implementation: Confronting complexity* (pp. 83 – 104). State University of New York Press.

Marginson, S., & Considine, M. (2000). *The enterprise university: Power, governance and reinvention in Australia.* New York: Cambridge University Press.

Massy, W. F., Wilger, A. K., & Colbeck, C. (1994). Overcoming hollowed collegiality. *Change, 26* (4), 10 – 20.

Maynard-Moody, S., & Leland, (1999). Stories from the front lines of public management: Street-level workers as responsible actors. In J. L. Brudney, L. J. O'Toole, H. G. Rainey, Jr. (Eds.). *Advancing public management: New developments in theory, methods, and practice* (pp. 109 – 126), Washington, DC: Georgetown University Press.

Maxwell, J. A. (1996). *Qualitative research design: An interpretive approach.* Thousand Oaks, CA: Sage.

McCowan, T. (2007). Expansion without equity: An analysis of current policy on access to higher education in Brazil. *Higher Education, 53*, 579 – 598.

McLendon, M. K., Heller, D. E., Young, S. P. (2005). State postsecondary policy innovation: Politics, competition, and the interstate migration of policy ideas. *The Journal of Higher Education, 76* (4), 363 – 400.

McNeely, C. L. (1995). Prescribing national educational policies: The role of international organizations. *Comparative Education Review, 39* (4), 483 – 507.

McNeely, C. L., & Cha, Y. K. (1994). Worldwide educational convergence through international organizations: Avenues for research. *Education Policy Analysis Achieves, 2* (14).

Meek, V. L. (1988). Institutional mergers in Australian higher education. In L. C. J. Goedegebuure & V. L. Meek (Eds.), *Change in higher education: The non-university sector*. Culemborg, the Netherland: Lemma.

Merriam, S. B. (1998). *Qualitative research and case study applications in education*. San Francisco: Jossey-Bass.

Miles, M., & Huberman, A. (1994). *Qualitative data analysis: An expanded sourcebook* (2nd ed.). Thousand Oaks, CA: Sage.

Mills, M. R. (2007). Stories of politics and policy: Florida's higher education governance reorganization. *Journal of Higher Education*, 78 (2), 162 – 187.

Min, W. F. (1991). Higher education finance in China: Current constraints and strategies for the 1990s. *Higher Education*, 21 (2), 151 – 161.

Min, W. F., & Ding, X. H. (1993). The economy of scale of higher education: An empirical study on types and quality. *Education Economics*, 1, 16 – 22.

Ministry of Education. (1985, May 27). Central government's decisions on the reform of educational system. Retrieved September 7, 2009 from http://www.moe.edu.cn/edoas/website18/18/info3318.htm

Ministry of Education. (1993, February 13). An outline of Chinese educational reform and development. Retrieved February 5, 2009, from http://www.moe.gov.cn/edoas/website18/level3.jsp? tablename = 208&infoid = 3334

Ministry of Education. (1998, December 24). *Action plan on revitalizing education for 21st Century*. Retrieved September 7, 2009 from http://www.moe.edu.cn/edoas/website18/37/info3337.htm

Ministry of Education. (1999). The higher education law. Retrieved April 28, 2010 from http://www.moe.gov.cn/edoas/website18/26/info1426.htm

Ministry of Education. (2002, June 6). The tenth five-year plan on education. Retrieved April 28, 2010 from http://www.

moe. edu. cn/edoas/website18/36/info3336. htm

Ministry of Education. (2004a, September). Introduction to 211 project. Retrieved February 5, 2009, from http://www. moe. gov. cn/edoas/website18/level3. jsp? tablename = 724&infoid = 5607

Ministry of Education. (2004b). The Q & A on the evaluation policies and methodologies on university teaching. Retrieved February 28, 2010 from http://www. gdin. edu. cn/pg/wj/%B3%A3%BC%FB%CE%CA%CC%E2%CE%CA%B4%F01. pdf

Ministry of Education. (2004c). A proposal on undergraduate teaching evaluation at regular universities (tentative). Retrieved February 28, 2010, from http://www. moe. edu. cn/edoas/website18/level3. jsp? tablename = 603&infoid = 11052

Ministry of Education. (2006a, May 11) Wen Jiabao convenes the regular congressional meeting and listen to reports on higher education work. Retrieved April 28, 2010 from http://www. moe. edu. cn/edoas/website18/level3. jsp? tablename = 217&infoid = 19520

Ministry of Education. (2006b, May 15). The amalgmation of universities since 1990. Retrieved April 28, 2010 from http://www. moe. gov. cn/edoas/website18/level3. jsp? tablename = 621&infoid = 19558

Ministry of Education. (2009a). A list of regular higher education institution in China. Retrieved April 28, 2010 from http://www. moe. gov. cn/edoas/website18/level3. jsp? tablename = 1231048877547308&infoid = 1245739874200607

Ministry of Education. (2009b). Information on international students. Retrieved March 20, 2010, from http://www. moe. edu. cn/edoas/website18/level3. jsp? tablename = 1261364343113580&infoid = 1261558323135145

Ministry of Education. (2010). The 211 project and 985 project. Retrieved April 28, 2010 from http://www.moe.edu.cn/edoas/website18/level3.jsp? tablename = 1267342373750173&infoid = 1267343395704187

Mohrman, K. (2003, July). Higher education reform in Mainland Chinese universities: An American's perspective, Retrieved February 5, 2005, from http://sais-jhu.edu/Nanjing/downloads/Higher_Ed_in_China.pdf

Mohrman, K. (2005). Sino-American educational exchanges and the drive to create world-class universities. In C. Li (Ed.). *Birding minds across the pacific: U. S. -China education exchanges*, 1978 – 2003 (pp. 219 – 236). Lanham, MD: Lexington.

Mohrman, K. (2008). The emerging global model with Chinese characteristics. *Higher Education Policy*, *21*, 29 – 48.

Mok, K. H. (1997). Retreat of the state: Marketization of education in Pearl River Delta. *Comparative Education Review*, *41* (3), 260 – 276.

Mok, K. H. (2001). Education policy reform. In L. Wong (Ed.), *Market in Chinese social policy* (pp. 88 – 111). Gordonsville, VA: Palgrave Macmillan.

Mok, K. H. (2004). *Centralization and decentralization: Educational reforms and changing governance in chinese society*. Hong Kong, China: Kluwer Academic.

Mok, K. H. (2005a). Riding over socialism and global capitalism: Changing education governance and social policy paradigms in post-Mao China. *Comparative Education*, *41* (2), 217 – 242.

Mok, K. H. (2005b). Globalization and educational restructuring: University merging and changing governance in China, *Higher Education*, *50*, 57 – 88.

Mok, K. H. (2007a). Local response to a global agenda:

Changing state-education relations in Mainland China. In W. Tang & B. Holzner (Eds.). *Social change in contemporary china: C. K. Yang and the concept of institutional diffusion* (pp. 153 – 175). PA: University of Pittsburgh Press.

Mok, K. H. (2007b). Globalization, new education governance and state capacity in East Asia. *Globalization, Societies and Education*, 5 (1), 1 – 21.

Morley, L. (2002). A comedy of manners: Quality and power in higher education. In P. R. Trowler (Ed.). *Higher education policy and institutional change: Intentions and outcomes in turbulent environments* (pp. 126 – 141). Philadelphia: The Society for Research into Higher Education and Open University.

Morley, L. (2003). *Quality and power in higher education*. Philadelphia: The Society for Research into Higher Education and Open University.

Newton, J. (2002). Views from below: Academics coping with quality. *Quality in Higher Education*, 8 (1), 39 – 61.

Nonaka, I. (1994). A dynamic theory of organizational knowledge creation. *Organization Science*, 5 (1), 14 – 37.

O'Connor, E. S. (1995). Paradoxes of participation: Textual analysis and organizational change. *Organization Studies*, 16, 769 – 803.

Ochs, E., & Capps, L. (2001). *Living narratives: Creating lives in everyday storytelling*. Cambridge, MA: Harvard University Press.

Olssen, M. (2004). Neoliberalism, globalization, democracy: Challenges for education. *Globalisation, Societies and Education*, 2 (2), 231 – 275.

Ordorika, I. (2003). The limits of university autonomy: Power and politics at the Universidad Nacional Automoma de Mexico, *Higher Education*, 46, 361 – 388.

Organization for Economic Co-operation and Development. (2003). OECD review of financing and quality assurance reforms in higher education in the People's Republic of China. Retrieved February 28, 2010 from http://www.oecd.org/dataoecd/40/33/17137038.pdf

Owens, R. G. (1998). *Organizational behavior in education*. Boston: Allyn and Bacon.

Pan, S. (2007). Intertwining of academic and officialdom and university autonomy: Experience from Tsinghua University in China. *Higher Education Policy*, *20*, 122 – 144.

Pan, W. (2004). The best does not have to be the largest; Questioning university amalmgation. *Learning Monthly*, *6*, 33 – 34.

Patton, M. Q. (2002). *Qualitative research evaluation methods*. Thousand Oaks, CA: Sage.

Pepper, S. (1996). *Radicalism and education reform in 20th-century China: The search for an ideal development model*. New York: Cambridge University Press.

Peters, M. (1992). Performance and accountability in "post-industrial society": The crisis of British universities. *Studies in Higher Education*, *17* (2), 123 – 139.

Power, M. (1997). *The audit society: Rituals of verification*. New York: Oxford University Press.

Ranson, S. (2003). Public accountability in the age of neoliberal governance. *Journal of Education Policy*, *18* (5), 459 – 480.

Rein, M., & Schön, D. (1993). Reframing policy discourse. In F. Fischer & J. Forester (Eds.). *The argumentative turn in policy analysis and planning* (pp. 145 – 166). Durham, NC: Duke University Press.

Rein, M., & Schön, D. (1996). Frame-critical policy analysis and frame reflective policy practice. *Knowledge, Technology and Policy*, *9* (1), 85 – 104.

Reinharz, S. (1997). Who am I: The need for a variety of selves in the field. In R. Hertz (Ed.). *Reflexivity and voice* (pp. 3–20). Thousand Oaks, CA: Sage.

Research Team at Beijing University. (2001). A research report on the impact of university expansion on the short-term economic growth. Retrieved September 4, 2009, from http://www.edu.cn/zong_he_311/20060323/t20060323_12479.shtml

Rhodes, C., & Brown, A. D. (2005). Narrative, organizations and research. *International Journal of Management Review*, 7 (3), 167–188.

Rhoades, G., & Sporn, B. (2002). Quality assurance in Europe and the U.S.: Professional and political economics framing of higher education policy. *Higher Education*, 43, 355–390.

Rodriguez, A. (2002). Redefining our understanding of narrative. *The Qualitative Report*, 7 (1), retrieved 12/31/2007 from http://www.nova.edu/ssss/QR/QR7-1/rodriguez.html

Sabatier, P. (2005). From policy implementation to policy change: A personal Odyssey. In A. Gornitzka, M. Kogan, & A. Amaral (Eds.). *Reform and change in higher education: Analyzing policy implementation* (pp. 17–34). Dordrecht, The Netherlands: Springer.

Sanger, P. C. (2003). Living and writing feminist ethnographies: Threads in a quilt stitched from the heart. In R. P. Clair (Ed.). *Expressions of ethnography: Novel approaches to qualitative methods* (pp. 141–151). Albany, NY: State University of New York.

Scott, A., & Harding, A. (2007). Introduction: Universities, "relevance" and scale. In A. Harding, A. Scott, S. Laske, C. Burtscher, (Eds.). *Bright satanic mills: Universities, regional development and the regional economy* (pp. 1–24). Burlington, VT: Ashgate.

References

Schön, D. A., & Rein, M. (1994). *Frame reflection: Toward the resolution of intractable policy controversies*. New York: Basic Books.

Seidman, I. (2006). *Interview as qualitative research: A guide for researchers in education and the social sciences*. New York: Teachers College.

Shambaugh, D. (2004/2005). China engages Asia: Reshaping the regional order. *International Security*, *29*(3), 64–99.

Shen, Y. S. (2006). Reflections and suggestions on the undergraduate teaching evaluation. *Research in Educational Development*, *19*, 1–4.

Shore, C., & Wright, S. (1999). Audit culture and anthropology: Neoliberalism in British higher education. *The Journal of Royal Anthropological Institute*, *5*, 557–575.

Shore, C., & Wright, S. (2000). Coercive accountability: The rise of audit culture in higher education. In M. Strathern (Ed.). *Audit cultures: Anthropological studies in accountability, ethics and the academy* (pp. 57–89). New York: Routledge.

Simmons, R. (2003, January 18). How to make a world-class university. *South China Morning Post*, p. 1.

Slaughter, S., & Leslie, L. L. (1997). *Academic capitalism: Politics, policies and the entrepreneurial university*. Baltimore, MD: John Hopkins University Press.

Slaughter, S., & Rhoades, G. (2004). *Academic capitalism and the new economy: Markets, state, and higher education*. Baltimore: MD: The John Hopkins University Press.

Sleeboom, M. (2004). *Academic nations in China and Japan: Framed in concepts of nature, culture and the universal*. London: RoutledgeCurzon.

Song, W. C., & Liao, Y. H. (2004). A political analysis on competitions among universities: Using the "985 Project" as an example. *The Journal of Higher Education*, 25 (6), 25 – 30.

Stake, R. E. (1995). *The art of case study research*. Thousand Oak, CA: Sage.

Stone, D. (2002). *Policy paradox: The art of political decision making*. New York: W. W. Norton.

Su, Z. S. (2000). Educational savings: Advantages and disadvantages. *Market Research*, 2, 38 – 39.

Sweetland, S. R. (1996). Human capital theory: Foundation of a field of inquiry. *Review of Educational Research*, 66 (3), 341 – 359.

Tang, M., & Zuo, X. L. (1999a, June 4). Boosting consumption through education is just about to be realized. *Economics News*, p. 1.

Tang, M., & Zuo, X. L. (1999b, October 15). Thinking in old ways does not create demands or supplies. *Economics News*, pp. 1, 4.

Tao, J. L. (2002). Differentiated evaluations on universities' research performance: Also discussing the usage of SCI. *Forum on Sciense and Technology in China*, 4, 53 – 54.

Task Force on Higher Education and Society. (2000). *Higher education in developing countries: Peril and promise*. Washington DC: World Bank.

Tatkirm S., Rizvi, F, Lingard, B., & Henry, M. (1997). *Educational policy and the politics of change*. London: Rutledge.

Teixeira, P., Jongboled, B., Dill, D., Amaral, A. (Eds.). *Markets in higher education: Rhetoric or reality*. Dordrecht, Netherlands: Kluwer Academic.

Tian, Z. J. (2006). The historical evoluation of the appraisement and engagement system of the professional title of China's college and university teachers. *Journed of Hunan University of Science and Engineering*, 27 (3), 265 – 268.

Torres, C. A., & Rhoads, R. A. (2006). Introduction: Globalization and higher education in the Americas. In R. A. Rhoads & C. A. Torres (Eds.). *The university, state, and market: The political economy of globalization in the Americas* (pp. 3 – 38). CA: Stanford University Press.

Torres, C. A., & Schugurensky, D. (2002). The political economy of higher education in the era of neoliberal globalization: Latin America in comparative perspective. *Higher Education, 43* (4), 429 – 455.

Trow, M. (1973). *Problems in the transition from elite to mass higher education* (Report No. 94704). Berkeley, CA: Carnegie Commission on Higher Education (ERIC Document Reproduction Service No. ED091983).

Trow, M. (1994). *Managerialism and the academic profession: Quality and control* (Higher Education Report No. 2). Milton Keynes, England: The Open University, Quality Support Center.

Trow, M. (1996a). *Trust, markets and accountability in higher education: A comparative perspective* (Research and Occasional Paper Series: CSHE. 1. 96). Berkley, CA: University of California, Center for Studies in Higher Education.

Trow, M. (1996b). On the accountability of higher education in the United States. In W. G. Bowen, & H. T. Shapiro. (Eds.). *Universities and their Leadership* (pp. 15 – 64). NJ: Princeton University Press.

Trowler, P. R. (1998). *Academics responding to change: New higher education frameworks and academic cultures.* Buckingham, England: SRHE and Open University.

Trowler, P. R. (2002). Introduction: Higher education policy, institutional change. In P. R. Trowler (Ed.). *Higher education policy and institutional change: Intentions and outcomes in turbulent environments* (pp. 1 – 23). Buckingham, MK: The Society for research into higher education and Open

University Press.

Trowler, P. R. (2005). A sociology of teaching, learning and enhancement: Improve practices in higher education. *Revista de Sociologia*, *76*, 13 - 32.

Tsang, M. C., & Min, W. F. (1992). Expansion, efficiency, and economies of scale of higher education in Chin. *Higher Education Policy*, *5* (2), 61 - 66.

UNESCO Institute For Statistics. (n. d.). Key statistic tables: Table 14 tertiary indicators. Retrieved April 28, 2010 from http://stats. uis. unesco. org/unesco/TableViewer/tableView. aspx? ReportId = 167

Vandenberghe, V. (1999). Combining market and bureaucratic control in education: An answer to market and bureaucratic failure? *Comparative Education*, *35* (3), 271 - 282.

Vidovich, L. (2002). Quality assurance in Australian higher education: Globalisation and "steering at a distance". *Higher Education*, *43*, 391 - 408.

Vidovich, L., Yang, Y., & Currie, J. (2007). Changing accountabilities in higher education as China 'opens up' to globalization. *Globalization, Societies and Education*, *5* (1), 89 - 107.

Waite, D., & Allen, D. (2003). Corruption and power abuse in educational administration. *The Urban Review*, *35* (4), 281 - 296.

Wan, Y. M. (2008). *Managing post-merger integration: A case study of a merger in Chinese higher education*. Unpublished doctoral dissertation, University of Michigan.

Wan, Y. M., & Peterson, M. W. (2007). A case study of a merger in Chinese higher education: The motives, processers and outcomes. *International Journal of Educational Development*, *27* (6), 683 - 696.

Wang, F., & Hu X. Y. (2009). Recognition and reflection on

undergraduate teaching evaluation in universities. *Journal of Hunan First Normal university*, *9* (3), 48−50.

Wang, H. C. (2004). *On mass higher education: Study on the orientation of culture-individuality of higher education massification.* Guangzhou, China: Guangdong Education Publishing House.

Wang, J. (2007). Analyzing the paths to cultural rebuilding of the amalgamated universities. *Jiangsu Higher Education*, *3*, 64−65.

Wang, N. (2006). On the recognition and defense of the current evaluative system of social science and humanity disciplines. *Academic Research*, *3*, 5−9.

Wang, P. J. (1996). Ten questions on university amalgamation. *Teacher Education Research*, *2*, 16−19.

Wang, Q., & Lin, J. (2005). A study of employees' satisfaction rate towards amalgamation at universities. *Theory and Practice of Education*, *25* (4), 36−38.

Wang, R. J. (2003). From elitism to mass higher education in Taiwan: The problems faced. *Higher Education*, *46* (3), 261−287.

Wang, X. F. (2003). *Education in China since 1976.* Jefferson, NC: McFarland.

Wang, Y. (2001). *Higher education reform in China.* Unpublished doctoral dissertation, Baylor University, Texas.

Wang, T., & Liu, X. M. (2006). *Exploring the experiences of overseas students in China.* Paper presented at the 2006 annual conference of the Association of Active Educational Researchers, Adelaid, Australia.

Wang, T., & Zeng, X. Q. (2009). An analysis on the cost of the structural unemployment of undergraduates and its solutions. *Education and Economy*, *1*, 1−4.

Weick, K. E. (1976). Educational organizations as loosely coupled systems. *Administrative Science Quarterly*, *21* (1), 1−19.

Weick, K. E. (1995). *Sensemaking in organizations.* Thousand Oaks, CA: Sage.

Went, R. (2000). *Globalisation: Neoliberal challenge, radical responses.* London: Pulto.

Weston, T. B. (2004). *The power of position: Beijing university, intellectuals and Chinese political culture*, 1898 – 1929. Berkeley, CA: University of California Press.

World Bank. (1986). China: Management and finance of higher education (Report No. PUB5912). Retrieved April 28, 2010 from http://www-wds. worldbank. org/external/default/ WDSContentServer/WDSP/IB/2000/07/19/000009265 3980716172030/Rendered/PDF/multi_page. pdf

Wu, J. L., & Fan, S. T. (2007). Establishing a mechanism that enhances the prosperity of scholarship and innovations in technologies: Some reflections on science development and technological innovations. In Z. G. Yuan (Ed.). *Review on educational policies* (pp. 3 – 11). Beijing, China: Education Science Publishing House.

Wu, K. M., & Lai, D. S. (2004). An economic analysis on university graduates' voluntary unemployment, *Jourual of Higher Education*, 25 (2), 38 – 41.

Wu, K. M., & Sun, B. C. (2005). An economic analysis on university graduates' unrealistic career expectations. *Education and Economy*, 4, 52 – 55.

Xie, K. Y. (2003). Perceiving university expansion from an economic perspective. *Modern Education Science*, 4, 39 – 41.

Xie, R. Y. (2004). On a dialogue between an age of university amalgamation and an age of post-university-amalgamation: A comparative study of Chinese and Japanese university amalgamation. *Fudan Education Forum*, 2 (1), 61 – 64.

Xiong, M. A. (1995). Reflecting and commenting on the several times of restructuring of universities in our country. *Journal of*

Higher Education, *4*, 48 – 55.

Xiong, X. M. (2005). The balance and relationship between bureaucratic power and academic power at universities in our country. *Design Research*, *24* (1), 13 – 15.

Xu, L. (2003). An economic analysis of the university merger: A case study of the merger of Fudan University and Shanghai Medical University. *China Higher Education Elualuation*, *1*, 18 – 22.

Xu, J. (2006). On the World Bank's impacts on Chinese universities' autonomous policies in a market controlling system. *Jiangsu Higher Education*, *4*, 13 – 16.

Yan, G. F., & Chang, Q. H. (2008). An analysis on the policy process of university expansion policy. *Journal of Higher Education Management*, *2* (3), 44 – 50.

Yang, C. L. (2007). On the inception and termination of university expansion policy in our country. *Journal of Yunnan Minzu University*, *24* (2), 151 – 153.

Yang, M. (2006). On the role and malfunction of government in higher education. *Journal of Zhejiang University*, *36* (4), 32 – 41.

Yang, R. (2002). *The third delight: The internationalization of higher education in China.* New York: Routledge.

Yang, R. (2004). Progress and paradoxes: New developments in China's higher education. In K. H. Mok (Ed.), *Centralization and decentralization: Education reforms and changing governance in Chinese society* (pp. 173 – 200). Hong Kong, China: Kluwer Academic.

Yang, R., Vidovich, L. & Currie, J. (2007). "Dancing in a cage": Changing autonomy in Chinese higher education. *Higher Education*, *54*, 575 – 592.

Yanow, D. (1996). *How does a policy mean? Interpreting policy and organizational actions.* Washington, DC: Georgetown

University Press.

Yanow, D. (2002). *Conducting interpretive policy analysis*. Thousand Oaks, CA: Sage.

Yanow, D. (2006). Introduction. In D. Yanow & P. Schwartz-Shea (Eds.). *Interpretation and method: Empirical research methods and the interpretive turn*. New York: M. E. Sharpe.

Ye, M., & Xiao, N. (2007). *Review of hot issues on higher education in China*. Beijing, China: China Science Publishing and Media.

Yin, C. F., & Xia, M. (2003). A comparative analysis on the difference of administrative power and academic power. *Journal of Jiangsu University*, *25*, 12–15.

Yin, R. (2003). *Application of case study research*. Thousand Oaks, CA: Sage.

Yogev, A. (2007). The stratification of students in Israeli universities: Persistent outcomes of an educational expansion policy. *Higher Education*, *54*, 629–645.

Yonezawa, A. (2007). Japanese flagship universities at crossroads. *Higher Education*, *54*, 483–499.

Yu, T. Z., & Xie, A. B. (2008). Reviews on undergraduate teaching evaluation research. *University*, *9*, 52–56.

Yuan, B. T., & Jiang, C. G. (2000). On university brandname: Also on the emergence of China's universities and the establishment of top-grade universities in the world, *Science and Technology Reviews*, *7*, 27–30.

Zeng, X. Q. (2004). Job seeking of college graduates in employment environment under transition. *Economic Research Journal*, *6*, 87–95.

Zeng, X. Q., & Niu, L. (2009). On the ability and strategies of undergraduates to take up careers. *China University Students' Career Guide*, *4*, 29–31.

Zha, Q. (2009). Diversification or homogenization: How governments and markets have combined to (re) shape Chinese higher education in its recent massification process. *Higher Education*, *58*, 41 – 58.

Zhang, G. Y. & Luo, Y. (2007). On the problems about our country's prizing system for science and technology, *Study in Sciences of Science*, *25* (2), 250 – 253.

Zhang, J. L. (2009). Relation between teaching and quality: Assumptions underlying the first round of undergraduate teaching assessment in China. *Modern University Education*, *3*, 98 – 105.

Zhang, J. N. (2006, May 11). Review of the book Bridging minds across the Pacific: U. S. -China educational exchanges, 1978—2003. *Education Review*, http://edrev. asu. edu/reviews/rev490. htm

Zhang, J. N. (2009). Mandarin maintenance among immigrant children from the People's Republic of China: The examination of Individual Network of Linguistic Contact. *Language, Culture and Curriculum.* *22* (3), 195 – 213.

Zhang, J. N. (2010, May). *Teaching and research accountability measures and their limitations at Chinese universities.* Paper presented at the 2010 Annual Meeting of American Education Research Association, Denver, CO.

Zhang, J. N. (2010). Parental attitudes towards Mandarin maintenance in Arizona: The examination of a group of immigrants from the People's Republic of China. *Critical Inquiry in Language Studies.* *7* (4), 237 – 269.

Zhang, N. M., & Zhou, Y. M. (2007). A few thoughts on the directions of reforms on faculty promotions in our country. *Modern University Education*, *9*, 251 – 253.

Zhang, Q., & Pang Q. S. (2004). Tracing and reflecting on the history of university amalgamation since the establishment of the People's Republic of China. *Modern University Education*,

1, 81 – 84.

Zhao, F. (1998). A remarkable move of restructuring: Chinese higher education. *Education Policy Analysis Archives*, 6 (5).

Zhao, S. (2007). An analysis of the current implementation of the educational policies in our country. *Forum on Contemporary Education*, *9*, 9 – 12.

Zhou, L. (2000a). University amalgamation and the building of modern university system. *Higher Education Exploration*, *4*, 40 – 56.

Zhou, L. (2000b). Case studies on multi-campus universities in China and abroad. *Journal of Higher Education*, 22 (2), 61 – 64.

Zhou, M. (2007). The equality and fairness of education: A reflection on the influences of public policies, through analysis of university expansion policy. *Journal of Northeast Normal University*, *6*, 175 – 179.

Zhu, K. X. (1995, November 24). Actively pushing forward the reform of higher education system, *Chinese Education Daily*, 1 – 2.

Zhu, R. J. (1999, June 18). Speech at the third national meeting on educational work (selected). Retrieved April 28, 2010 from http://www.tech.net.cn/info/open/middle/90.shtml